GLOBET

Trave

C000148277

TEL AVIV AND JERUSALEM

SUE BRYANT

NEW
HOLLAND

NEW
HOLLAND

★★★ Highly recommended
★★ Recommended
★ See if you can

Second edition published in 2012
by New Holland Publishers (UK) Ltd
London • Cape Town • Sydney • Auckland
10 9 8 7 6 5 4 3 2 1

website: www.newhollandpublishers.com

Garfield House, 86 Edgware Road
London W2 2EA
United Kingdom

Wembley Square, First Floor
Solan Street, Gardens
Cape Town 8001 South Africa

Unit 1, 66 Gibbes Street
Chatswood NSW 2067
Australia

218 Lake Road
Northcote, Auckland
New Zealand

Distributed in the USA by
The Globe Pequot Press, Connecticut

This guidebook has been written by independent authors
and updaters. The information therein represents their
impartial opinion, and neither they nor the publishers
accept payment in return for including in the book or
writing more favourable reviews of any of the establishments. Whilst every effort has been made to ensure that this
guidebook is as accurate and up to date as possible, please
be aware that the facts quoted are subject to change, particularly the price of food, transport and accommodation.
The Publisher accepts no responsibility or liability for
any loss, injury or inconvenience incurred by readers or
travellers using this guide.

Publishing Manager: Thea Grobbelaar
DTP Cartographic Manager: Genené Hart
Editor: Thea Grobbelaar
Design and DTP: Nicole Bannister
Cartographers: Reneé Spocter, Genené Hart
Consultant: Andrew Sanger

Reproduction by Resolution, Cape Town
Printed and bound by Times Offset (M) Sdn. Bhd., Malaysia

Acknowledgements:
The author would like to thank BMI and Dan Hotels for
their support during the research of this book.

Photographic credits:
Jon Arnold/awl-images.com: pages 19, 78, 80, 94, 104,
112; **Hanan Isachar/awl-images.com:** pages 11, 98, 119;
Travel Pix Collection/awl-images.com: page 56; **Sue
Bryant:** pages 12, 35, 38, 42, 45, 50, 51, 52, 58, 60, 75,
81, 107, 113; **Adrian Baker/International PhotoBank:**
page 116; **Digital Source/Cubo Images:** page 25; **Digital
Source/Image Broker:** page 32; **Digital Source/SIME:**
page 30; **Larry Luxner:** page 16; **Dinu Mendrea:** cover;
Travel Pictures Ltd: title page, pages 4, 6, 8, 10, 20, 23,
24, 26, 27, 28, 29, 46, 48, 53, 61, 63, 64, 68, 72, 76, 84,
86, 87, 88, 89, 92, 101, 102, 106, 109, 110, 120;
Berthold Werner: page 95.

Keep us Current
Information in travel guides is apt to change, which is
why we regularly update our guides. We'd be grateful to
receive feedback if you've noted something we should
include in our updates. If you have new information,
please share it with us by writing to the Publishing
Manager, Globetrotter, at the office nearest to you
(addresses on this page). The most significant contri-
bution to each new edition will receive a free copy
of the updated guide.

Front cover: *Hassan Bet Mosque, Tel Aviv.*
Title page: *Basilica of the Holy Sepulchre, Jerusalem.*

CONTENTS

1
Introducing Tel Aviv and Jerusalem

Two cities, located just a short way apart but separated by millennia of history. **Tel Aviv**, young, secular, energetic, cosmopolitan; and **Jerusalem**, serious and contemplative, its ancient stones having witnessed three thousand years of struggle for dominance between three of the world's great faiths.

Tel Aviv basks on some of the Mediterranean's finest **beaches**; Jerusalem, glowing gold as it reclines gently over the ancient **Judean Hills**, perches on the **fault-line** of the ongoing Israeli-Palestinian conflict, serene yet controversial.

Tel Aviv is Israel's epicentre of fine **cuisine**, artistic creativity and one of the hottest **nightlife** scenes around the Mediterranean. Jerusalem, although no stranger to the arts itself, is best known for its magnetic draw to both believers and non-believers, anxious to unpeel layer upon layer of **history**, searching for a **spiritual connection**.

Jerusalem is packed solid with ancient sites, each more breathtaking than the last, from the **Via Dolorosa**, where Christians believe Jesus to have taken his final steps, to the **Western Wall**, the holiest of Jewish places.

Tel Aviv has no such heritage, being a mere 100 years old, but the towering blocks of hotels and expensive condos lining the beachfront conceal leafy streets lined with the world's finest collection of **Bauhaus** architecture, the legendary **White City**. At the southern end of the beach is ancient **Jaffa**, predating Jerusalem by centuries and today a thriving **cultural centre**.

TOP ATTRACTIONS

★★★ **Jerusalem's Old City:** thousands of years of history.
★★★ **Yad Vashem:** the moving Holocaust Memorial.
★★★ **Israel Museum:** home of some of the Dead Sea Scrolls.
★★★ **The White City:** Tel Aviv's beautiful Bauhaus architecture.
★★★ **Jaffa Port:** wonderful nightlife and restaurants.

Opposite: *One of the enticing markets in the labyrinth of streets that forms the Old City of Jerusalem.*

No visit to Israel would be complete without taking in both Tel Aviv and Jerusalem, whatever your faith or reason for visiting. Each will assault your senses, surprise you, educate you and leave an indelible impression. Without even trying, these cities are addictive, fascinating and life-changing.

Above: *Snow on the rooftops of Jerusalem is a relatively rare sight.*

THE LAND

Tel Aviv and Jerusalem are the two largest cities of Israel, a country of incredible natural diversity – Tel Aviv basking on the sunny coastal plain alongside long, sandy Mediterranean beaches, Jerusalem lying some 63km (39 miles) southeast of here, sprawling over the arid Judean Hills.

Snowcapped mountains, arid hills, desert, green vineyards and rocky hills all fall within the compact boundaries of Israel as a whole, although the two cities have naturally been built away from any geographical extremes. The country is just 418km (260 miles) from north to south and 112km (70 miles) at its widest point. Physical borders are formed by the **Mediterranean Sea** to the west, the northernmost fragments of the **Great Rift Valley** to the east, and a narrow finger of the **Red Sea** in the south. Israel shares its political borders with Lebanon, Syria, Jordan, Egypt and the Palestinian Territory.

Mountains and Rivers

The snowcapped **Mount Hermon** in the **Golan Heights** to the north is the country's highest point, at 2224m (7296ft). A lower, undulating range forming the Hills of Galilee, Samaria and Judea creates the spine of the

---

ISRAEL'S WATER

Most of Israel's water for drinking and irrigation comes from the Sea of Galilee. With thousands of tourists a year, salt springs, peat flows and sewage from the area to contend with, the lake's ecosystem is increasingly fragile. The water is dangerously close to its 'red line', the line below which its pollutants become too concentrated for consumption. Israelis are used to conserving water and visitors should respect the notices in hotels asking them to do the same.

northern end of the country; Jerusalem is built in the Judean Hills. The **Jordan River**, which links the Sea of Galilee – in reality an inland lake – with the Dead Sea, forms the lifeblood of Israel. Fed by three tributaries, **Nahal Hermon** (a spring at the base of Mount Hermon), **Nahal Dan** and **Nahal Senir** from the Lebanon, the river gushes into the Sea of Galilee from the north. The **Yarkon River**, on the banks of which Tel Aviv is situated, is the country's longest coastal waterway, emerging as a series of springs in Yarkon National Park near Tel Aviv. It is possible to cycle the 28km (17 miles) from there to Ha-Yarkon Park in the city and the mouth of the river by Tel Aviv's **New Port**.

Jerusalem spills over a series of low hills: the **Mount of Olives**, **Mount Herzl**, **Mount Scopus** and **Mount Zion**. Its water supply once came from underground springs emerging in the **Kidron Valley** and there's a complex system of wells and channels under the Old City.

Climate

Summer in Israel extends all the way from April to October, with short, mild winters from November to March. Tel Aviv in summer is fanned by sea breezes, with an average daily maximum of 30°C (86°F) in August and September, the hottest and most humid months. Summer temperatures in Jerusalem reach 19–29°C (66–84°F); there's less breeze, but less humidity too.

Winters here are cool, with January temperatures dropping to around 6°C (42°F) in Jerusalem and sometimes lower, causing ground frost and even snow. Tel Aviv enjoys mild winters; you'll see people windsurfing in January.

Plant Life

Thanks to its incredibly diverse landscape, Israel supports an astonishing variety of animals and plants. This was not always the case; under the rule of the **Ottoman Turks**, mass deforestation meant the land became a dust bowl and many birds and mammals became extinct. The **Jewish National Fund** has set up a huge

---

SEASONS IN JERUSALEM

In March and April, almond blossom is pink on the trees and the roadsides are lined with scarlet poppies. This is prime time for hiking and walking in the hills and national parks around the city. By summer, grapes are fat on the vines and the country roads are lined with stalls selling cantaloupe and watermelons. Evenings are spent recovering from the heat of the day, dining on outdoor terraces. By autumn the weather is cooler, and as winter looms, citrus fruit comes into season, the trees heavy with lemons, limes and oranges. Huge piles of pomegranates appear in the markets. In January or February, it may even rain – an event greeted with cheers of joy from the locals.

GEOGRAPHY AND STATISTICS

Independence day: 14 May 1948
Members of parliament: 120
Population: 7.47 million
Religion: 80% Jews; the remaining 20% Muslims, Samaritans, Christians, Druze, Baha'i and others.
Languages: Hebrew and Arabic. English, French, German, Yiddish, Russian, Spanish, Polish and Hungarian are also spoken.
Highest point: Mount Hermon, 2224m (7296ft)
Lowest point: Dead Sea, about -400m (-1300ft)

SHIP OF THE DESERT

The camel is well adapted to its surroundings. The Arabian camel eats the thorny plants that grow in the desert and stores fat in its hump. It can survive for days without water. Thick, broad pads on its soles and calluses on the knees and chest, upon which the camel rests in a kneeling position, enable it to with-stand the heat of the sand. The camel can close its nos-trils against flying dust and its eyes are shielded by very long eyelashes. It can also cover more than 160km (100 miles) in a day. Its flesh and milk can be used as food, and its hide for leather, while its long hair, which is shed every summer, is made into fine brushes and camel-hair cloth.

Below: *Some of the olive trees in Jerusalem's Garden of Gethsemane are hundreds of years old.*

reforestation programme (this was started in the 1950s) which has resulted in around 10% of the country's land area being covered with trees.

Beautiful **forests** of Eurasian oak, African acacia, cypress and the native Jerusalem pine now cover Israel's soil, with oleander, myrtle and fragrant wild herbs flourishing in the drier areas. Cultivated trees include olive, apricot, almond, citrus and walnut.

Wildlife

Hundreds of species of **migratory birds** pass Israel en route from Europe to Africa, among them storks, herons, ducks, pelicans, hawks, gulls, waders, plovers, sandpipers, flamingoes and songbirds. Once every seven years, when the vineyards outside Tel Aviv are left fallow according to kosher law, the birds enjoy a free bonanza of ripe grapes.

In addition, the **Hai-bar** programme aims to bring back biblical creatures such as the addax antelope, the wild Asiatic ass (once ridden by Jesus), the Meso-potamian fallow deer, the exquisite white oryx (the creature which spawned the myth of the unicorn) and even ostrich to the land of the Bible. This means that more and more rare wild animals are being released in Israel's 280 nature reserves; or you can see them close up in the Jerusalem **Biblical Zoo**.

You won't spot much wildlife around Tel Aviv as it's highly urbanized. But if you visit **Ha-Yarkon Park**, some 28km (17 miles) from the city, you can look out for foxes, kingfishers with their brilliant turquoise wings, and the green flash of once-captive lovebirds.

HISTORY IN BRIEF

Situated at the crossroad of two continents, Africa and Asia, and passed by all the great trade routes of the ancient world, it was inevitable that the tiny sliver of land now called Israel should play a dramatic role in world history. Its location, combined with the belief of three great religions – **Christianity**, **Judaism** and **Islam** – in its spiritual importance, has inspired ceaseless years of struggle over the **land of milk and honey**.

The Land of Canaan

By 3000BC, Canaanite tribes had established fortified cities in this land which bordered the two great powers of the time, Egypt and Assyria, both of whom indulged in frequent, vicious battles along the Mediterranean trade route. New tribes began to arrive; belonging to one of these tribes was the patriarch **Abraham**, believed to have come from Ur in what is now Iraq and to have fathered the Israeli people. Although the only record of Abraham and his sons Isaac and Jacob is in the Bible (there is a possibility that Abraham himself was a mythical figure), there was certainly a leader of the Israelite tribe who, unlike the other tribes of the time, worshipped a single deity.

By the 13th century BC, Egypt had been weakened in the north by its war with the **Hittite Empire**, a feature of North Syria and Asia Minor during the second millennium BC, and gradually new, smaller powers including Abraham's descendants, the Israelites, began to emerge.

The Israelites and the Promised Land

According to the Bible, Abraham's descendants were taken into **slavery** in Egypt around 1550BC. The Book of Exodus tells how they escaped under the leadership of **Moses**, made a miraculous 40-year journey across the wilderness and the Red Sea, and received the **Ten Commandments** on Mount Sinai before conquering their Promised Land. The Israelites settled in what is now Israel during the early **Iron Age** (1200BC) and formed a monarchy, headed by **King Saul** whose adopted son and successor, David, led them to final victory over the

---

HEROD THE HATED

Herod the Great (73–4BC), the king of Judea from 37BC, was hated by the Jews who regarded him as a foreigner and a friend of the Romans. According to Matthew 2:16 Herod tried to kill the infant Jesus by massacring all the male babies in Bethlehem. Yet he also sought to consolidate his position with the Jews by marrying Mariamne, a princess of the Hasmonean line, whom he later killed. Herod is remembered for his defeat of Cleopatra and Mark Antony and also for his architectural projects, especially the rebuilding of the Jews' Holy Temple in Jerusalem.

ELIJAH'S CHALLENGE

Elijah was a popular Hebrew prophet, famous for his struggle against Ahab, the king who worshipped Baal, the Phoenician god.

According to the Bible, Elijah challenged the pagans to a contest of 'miracles' and stated that only he could command the rain. After three years of drought, Elijah assembled the people of Israel on Mount Carmel and said that he had proved his point. The Baal-worshipers were killed and sure enough, the rains came.

Right: *The original scrolls of the Torah were kept in the Ark of the Covenant, which was housed in the First Temple.*
Opposite: *The hilltop fortress of Masada was the scene of a tragic siege in AD66.*

THE BOOK OF EXODUS

The Book of Exodus is one of history's great adventure stories. It tells the story of God choosing Moses to lead the 'Children of Israel' out of slavery in Egypt. Ten plagues are inflicted on the Egyptians and the waters of the Red Sea part to allow the fleeing Israelites to cross.

Subsequently, in Sinai, while the Israelites are wandering in the wilderness, Moses encounters the burning bush. God then gives Moses the Ten Commandments and the Israelites build the Tabernacle on Mount Sinai into which are placed various sacred objects, among them the Ark of the Covenant. The Jewish feast of Sukkot today recreates the conditions of the wilderness as families eat under temporary shelters outside their homes.

Philistines, an aggressive race still controlling the coast. Saul himself secured many military victories, but it was David who conquered Jerusalem, proclaiming it the capital of the 12 tribes of Israel. His son, Solomon, built the **First Temple**, installing the **Ark of the Covenant** (which contained the two tablets of stone on which were carved the Ten Commandments) to be the focal point for Jewish worship.

By the time of **King Solomon** (950BC), Israel was a powerful land, stretching from the Red Sea to the Euphrates River in the north. But jealousies between tribes led to 10 in the north forming the Kingdom of Israel, while the tribes of Judah and Benjamin formed the southern Kingdom of Judea. Alliances with neighbours continued to be formed and broken until the northern kingdom fell in 722BC to invading Assyria.

Babylonian and Persian Rule

The Israelites from the north were exiled overseas and gradually became absorbed into other societies. The south held out for a further 150 years until the **Babylonians**, who had replaced the Assyrians in power, invaded in 586BC. The Babylonian army crushed Judah and defiled the Temple of Jerusalem. The surviving population was exiled to Babylonia, where they mourned for their lost land.

As foretold by the prophets of the time, the Babylonian Empire fell to Persians 40 years later and the exiles were allowed to return. The Temple of Jerusalem was rebuilt between 535 and 515BC but tension ran high between the **Jews** (from Judah) and the **Samaritans**, those northerners who had stayed in Israel and intermarried with foreign immigrants brought in by the Assyrians.

Roman Times

Alexander the Great defeated the Persians in 333BC and for 900 years the area known as Palestina was part of the Greco-Roman Empire. Hellenic rulers attempted to outlaw Judaism in the 2nd century BC, defiling the Temple in the process. Jewish sovereignty was then re-established, but lasted only until 63BC, when the country was annexed by the Romans. **Herod**, the ruler of the time, invested heavily in refurbishing the Temple. Jesus was born – and died – at the time when Jews were split into different factions: the wealthy Sadducees, the Pharisees, the Essenes, and fanatical Zealots.

United by a hatred for the Romans, the Jews revolted in AD66, only to be crushed three years later. The Temple was destroyed and the final Jewish Zealot stronghold, **Masada**, fell in AD73 with the mass suicide of its inhabitants. The Jewish population that remained around Galilee in the north rebelled again in AD132 but was broken once and for all by the Romans' sheer numbers. Villages were destroyed and many Jews were sold into slavery.

THE SCROLLS OF HISTORY

The **Dead Sea Scrolls** were discovered in 1947 by a Bedouin shepherd who was looking for a lost goat around the shores of the Dead Sea. In the ruined mountainous settlement of **Qumran**, once inhabited by the devout Essene people, the Bedouin threw a stone into a cave and heard the sound of pottery being smashed.

Further investigation revealed earthenware jars filled with flaking parchment, dating from between 100BC and AD100. Subsequent explorations revealed more scrolls and many fragments of pottery, most of which are now housed in the **Israel Museum**.

TERRORISM IN ISRAEL

Israel is under a constant threat from terrorism and visitors should take care when travelling in the Occupied Palestinian Territories including the West Bank. Visitors should remain vigilant at all times in Israeli cities. All non-essential travel to the Gaza Strip is strongly discouraged. Although Israel to an extent does live with the threat of attack, daily life goes on. You'll find X-ray machines and bag inspections at some public areas like the Western Wall, or nightclubs in Tel Aviv, but most people go about their daily business without undue worry.

Below: *The original Dome of the Rock, one of Jerusalem's most distinctive sights, was built in AD691.*

Diaspora

The Jews scattered far and wide, from Egypt to Eastern Europe, where they worked as traders. This became known as the **Diaspora**, the Greek word for 'dispersion'. As Christianity became the official religion of the Roman Empire, widespread hostilities against Jews began again, although a community in Babylon, away from the Christian areas, continued to thrive.

In the 7th century the Muslim religion, Islam, was founded by the prophet **Mohammed**. After receiving his first revelation in 616, Mohammed taught in Mecca, his teachings forming the basis of the Qur'an, Islam's sacred scripture. He was forced to flee to **Medina** in 622, but returned with his followers to conquer Mecca in 630, becoming the recognized prophet of Arabia.

Fuelled by this new religion, an Arab invasion took place in 640, their army storming across what was then Palestine and conquering it. Palestine became part of Syria and Jerusalem was declared a Holy City by the Muslims. The great mosque, the **Dome of the Rock**, was built in 691.

Crusades

Christians in Europe viewed the Arab rule of the Holy Land as an insult, and in the 11th century the **Pope** ordered a series of Crusades, which by 1099 had effectively reconquered Jerusalem, though thousands of Muslims and Jews were slaughtered in the process. After the Second Crusade (1147–49) Jews were allowed back into Jerusalem, but the Third and Fourth Crusades, ending in 1204, were particularly vicious and anti-Semitic, branding Jews as 'God-killers'.

HISTORICAL CALENDAR

12,000BC Cave-dwellers in Carmel.

7500BC Settlement in Jericho.

3200BC Canaanite tribes establish fortified cities.

2200–1500BC Abraham founds Hebrew race, Canaan.

1550–1200BC Exodus from Egypt. Delivery of the Ten Commandments (Mt Sinai).

1000BC Jerusalem becomes capital of 12 tribes of Israel.

960BC King Solomon builds First Temple.

722BC Northern kingdom falls to the Assyrians; the Jews are exiled.

586BC Babylonians destroy the Temple.

535–515BC Temple rebuilt.

332–37BC Hellenistic Period.

166–160BC Desecration of the Temple.

37–4BC Herod's rule. Refurbishment of the Temple.

AD20–33 Ministry and crucifixion of Jesus of Nazareth.

AD70 Destruction of Jerusalem by the Romans.

AD73 Fall of Masada.

4th Century AD Christianity becomes the official religion of the Roman Empire.

AD622 Birth of Islam; Muslim Arabs conquer the Middle East.

AD637 Jerusalem surrenders to the Arabs.

AD691 Dome of the Rock constructed.

1099–1291 Crusader Period; Jews massacred.

1291–1516 Mameluke rule.

1517–1917 Ottoman rule.

1860 First neighbourhoods built outside the Old City of Jerusalem.

1882 First wave of immigrants (*aliya*), from Russia.

1889 Opening of Suez Canal revives trade routes.

1897 First Zionist World Congress.

1909 City of Tel Aviv founded outside walls of Jaffa.

1914–18 World War I. Britain promises Palestinian Jews and Arabs liberation.

1917–48 British Mandate. Jewish immigration to Palestine restricted. Six million Jews murdered by the Nazis in World War II.

1948 State of Israel proclaimed. Immediate invasion by Arab armies. Israel divided.

1967 The Six Day War; Jerusalem reunited.

1973 Yom Kippur War.

1978 Egypt and Israel sign Camp David Accords.

1985 Israeli Defence Forces withdraw from Lebanon.

1987 Intifada, the Palestinian uprising. Terrorist attacks.

1990–91 Gulf War; PLO backs Iraq. Tel Aviv bombed.

1993 Peace agreement signed between Yitzhak Rabin and Yasser Arafat. Jericho and Gaza Strip under Palestinian self-government.

1994 Land border with Jordan opens at Eilat.

1995 Rabin assassinated.

1999 Likud Party elected.

2000 Second Intifada.

2001 Ariel Sharon elected prime minister.

2002 Israel launches Operation Defensive Shield and builds 'anti-terrorist' fence, cutting off Palestinian areas.

2004 Death of Yasser Arafat.

2005 Israeli settlers withdraw from Gaza.

July–Aug 2006 Second Lebanon War.

2007 Renewed Israeli military action in Gaza leads to more violence.

2009 Israel and Hamas announce cease-fire.

2010 Renewed threat of Israeli settlement construction on West Bank causes unrest.

2011 Palestinians make bid for full UN membership.

In 1187 **Saladin**, the ruler of Egypt, managed to rout the Crusaders at the Horns of Hittim and Jews were once again allowed to live in Jerusalem. A series of disastrous campaigns was carried out by the Crusaders in an attempt to recoup their losses, but in 1291 the Crusader kingdom finally came to an end with the fall of **Akko**, when the Crusaders were defeated by the Muslim Mamelukes who had succeeded Saladin as rulers of Egypt.

THE FATHER OF ZIONISM

Born in May 1860 in Budapest, **Theodor Herzl** is regarded as the Father of Zionism. He studied law in Vienna but ended up following a career as a journalist and playwright. Herzl grew increasingly concerned about the rise of anti-Semitism in Vienna in the 1880s – the initial motivation in Zionism was not to preserve a religion, but simply to protect Jewish people. In 1896 he published *The Jewish State*, a guide to creating a refuge for Jews. In 1897 he organized the first World Zionist Congress in Basel, Switzerland, and set up a Jewish Colonial Trust. He continued to lobby internationally for a home for the world's Jews until his death in 1904.

The region did not prosper under the **Mamelukes**, who ruled from 1291 to 1516. The port of Jaffa was largely destroyed for fear of further invasion and the Holy Land became a backwater. Jerusalem was mainly abandoned and poverty was rife.

Ottoman Conquest

The Ottoman ousted the Mamelukes in 1517 and divided the land into four districts which were ruled from Istanbul and administered from the province of Damascus. An estimated 5000 Jewish families lived in the country at this time, in Jerusalem, Nablus, Hebron, Gaza, Safed and the villages around Galilee – a mix of native Jews and immigrants from Spain. Once again, though, the decline in power of the Ottoman rulers left the region impoverished, the forests of Galilee and Carmel decimated, to be replaced by swampland and encroaching deserts.

Birth of Zionism

Then during the 19th century, everything changed. Missionary activity from overseas opened up the Holy Land and encouraged immigration. Trade began to thrive after the opening of the **Suez Canal** in 1889 and the first road was built from Jaffa to Jerusalem. The population expanded and the first neighbourhoods developed outside the city walls of Jerusalem. By the early 20th century, the port of Jaffa was so overcrowded it needed to expand beyond the walls, and in 1909 the city of **Tel Aviv** was established.

Meanwhile, life continued to be tough for the Jewish exiles. The **pogroms**, or mass persecution of the Jews in Russia, which caused tens of thousands of Jews to flee yet again – some of them to Palestine – gave rise to a new feeling: **Zionism**. This was the call for the establishment of a Jewish state in Palestine, first dreamed of by the Russian-born journalist **Peretz Smolenskin**. The idea was brought together by a Viennese journalist and playwright **Theodor Herzl** (1860–1904), who lobbied the influential to find a home for the scattered Jewish people. He published a document, *The Jewish State*, in 1896 and established the **World Zionist Congress** in 1897. In 1917, in the famous Balfour Declaration, British foreign minister Arthur Balfour promised that Britain would support the establishment of a 'Jewish national home' in Palestine. In the same year, British forces entered Jerusalem under **General Allenby**, ending 400 years of Ottoman rule.

The State of Israel

In July 1922, the League of Nations entrusted Great Britain with the **Mandate for Palestine**. It was decided, however, that the provisions for setting up a Jewish national home would not apply to the area east of the Jordan River, which accounted for three-quarters of the territory included in the Mandate. This region eventually became the Kingdom of Jordan.

Wave upon wave of refugees continued to descend on Palestine, threatened by the appointment of the Nazi **Adolf Hitler** as chancellor of Germany in 1933. There was increasing unrest and uprising by Palestinian Arabs, themselves nervous of the growing Jewish power in Palestine.

The British clamped down on immigration, divided between support of the Jews and their need to maintain economic relations with the Arabs. During World War II (1939–45), six million Jews were exterminated by the Nazis, yet the terrified refugees who tried to immigrate after the **Holocaust** continued to be turned away.

Three determined Jewish militias set out to force the British out of Palestine, each operating in their own way: the **Irgun** under Menachem Begin, its splinter group the **Lehi** under Avraham Stern, and the larger and longer-established **Haganah** organization which at times co-operated with the British. All used highly successful guerrilla operations, and the British instituted severe reprisals. In one of the best-known incidents, Begin's Irgun movement planted bombs in the British headquarters, the **King David Hotel** in Jerusalem, killing 91 people. In 1947 the United Nations voted to partition Palestine into a Jewish and an Arab state. The Arabs were outraged. The independent State of Israel was proclaimed on 14 May 1948 by its first prime minister, **David Ben-Gurion**.

Above: *The Declaration of Independence: the State of Israel came into being on 14 May 1948.*

Almost immediately, though, the celebrations ended as Egypt, Jordan, Syria, Lebanon and Iraq invaded the new country. In the ensuing seven-month War of Independence, Israel came out victorious but at the cost of 6000 lives. Negotiations for a settlement took place under the United Nations. The Coastal Plain, Galilee and the entire Negev were kept within Israel's sovereignty, Judea and Samaria (the West Bank) came under Jordanian rule, the Gaza Strip came under Egyptian administration, and the city of Jerusalem was divided, with Jordan controlling the eastern part, including the Old City, and Israel the western sector.

In July 1950, the **Law of Return** was passed by the first Knesset (parliament), granting all Jews the right to Israeli citizenship. More waves of mass immigration followed, along with extensive funding of the new state from Jews living in the worldwide Diaspora.

The new State of Israel remained a cause of concern to the Arab world, so much so that President Nasser of Egypt nationalized and assumed control of the Suez Canal which had been developed as a private company in which Britain and France were the majority shareholders.

France and Britain took military action in 1956 and in the course of events Israel extended her borders, claiming the Gaza Strip and the Sinai as hers. These territories, however, were relinquished to Egypt in the ceasefire agreement between the European powers.

Uncertain Times

Matters came to a head again in 1967, with a massive build-up of hostile troops along Israel's borders. After six days of fighting, previous cease-fire lines were replaced by new ones, with Judea, Samaria, Gaza, the Sinai Peninsula and the Golan Heights under Israel's control. Jerusalem, which had been divided under Israeli and Jordanian rule since 1949, was reunified under Israel's authority.

In 1973, several years of relative calm came to an end on **Yom Kippur** (the Day of Atonement), the holiest day of the Jewish year, when Egypt and Syria invaded Israel via the Suez Canal and the Golan Heights.

During the next three weeks, the **Israeli Defence Forces** turned the tide of battle and repulsed the attackers, crossing the Suez Canal into Egypt and advancing to within 32km (20 miles) of the Syrian capital, Damascus. It took two years of further negotiation before Israel withdrew.

In 1977, Egypt's President **Anwar Sadat** announced a desire for peace, and soon Begin extended the first olive branch to Sadat. In 1979 the Camp David Accords were signed, drawing up a framework for peace and self-government by the Palestinians. Israel withdrew from the Sinai.

However, ongoing fighting with Lebanon and sporadic episodes between Israel and the **Palestine Liberation Organization** (PLO) continued until 1985, when the last Israeli Defence Forces withdrew from Lebanon. A tentative peace settled for two years, until **Intifada**, a Palestinian uprising in Gaza and the West Bank, occurred. During the **Gulf War** (1990–91), the PLO sided with Iraq, and Israel feared attack by chemical weapons. Conventional missiles did hit Tel Aviv but Israel's lack of retaliation led to the establishment of diplomatic relations with a number of countries.

In September 1993 a new peace agreement was signed between **Yitzhak Rabin** and **Yasser Arafat** of the PLO. Under these Oslo Accords, Jericho and the Gaza Strip were granted a degree of Palestinian autonomy.

THE SEPARATION BARRIER

Israel's controversial Separation Barrier, known as the Apartheid Wall by the Palestinians, brutally cuts the landscape in half, slicing towns and individual streets in two. The wall, still under construction, is 620km (385 miles) long, with the proposed total length of around 800km (500 miles). Global organizations such as Amnesty International believe that the construction violates human rights as it cuts farmers off from their land, residents of villages from their relatives, and individual Palestinians from their places of work, from healthcare facilities and schools.

DESERT TOMBS

Israel's first prime minister, **David Ben-Gurion**, is buried in modest surroundings, deep in the Negev Desert, alongside his wife, Paula, close to the kibbutz where they spent their later years. Their tomb is in a national park (situated on the edge of an escarpment) where local stone and flora blend harmoniously into the barren wastes of the surrounding desert. The tomb is worth a visit for its superb views alone.

Above: *The Star of David forms the centre of the Israeli flag.*
Opposite: *Israel's parliament building, the Knesset, is situated in Jerusalem.*

Further cities were handed back to the Palestinians in 1994. In the same year, land borders opened between Jordan and the Israeli resort of Eilat in the south. However, Israeli Prime Minister Yitzhak Rabin was assassinated in November 1995 by a Jewish extremist and September 1996 saw further uprisings in Hebron and the Gaza Strip. In 2000, there was a **second Intifada** with Palestinian attacks on Israeli civilians, further hampering the peace process.

US president George W Bush was instrumental in the creation of a **Roadmap for Peace** in 2003, along with the UN, the EU and Russia, although it took until 2005 for this to have any significant impact. Meanwhile, in 2002, Israel began the construction of a massive security fence along areas bordering Palestinian territory, ostensibly as protection of its citizens against terrorism, but alienating many Palestinians from the peace process.

Israel disengaged from the Gaza Strip in the summer of 2005, evacuating its settlers and the IDF, although it maintained (and still does) control over the entry points. In 2006, the Palestinians elected **Hamas**, a Muslim extremist group, to head the Palestinian Legislative Council, which froze relations with Israel once again.

Ehud Olmert became Israel's prime minister in March 2006 and shelved plans to evacuate Israel's presence from most of the West Bank following an Israeli military operation in Gaza in June–July 2006 and a 34-day conflict with Hezbollah in Lebanon in June–August 2006.

Talks resumed with the Palestinian National Authority after Hamas seized control of the Gaza Strip and PA President **Mahmoud Abbas** formed a new government to oversee the West Bank without the Hamas militia. Ehud Olmert resigned in September 2008 and elections were

SERVING THEIR COUNTRY

The **Israeli Defence Force** (IDF) is a source of national pride. All men and women are required at the age of 18 to do national service. For men, this service lasts for three years but women are only required to do two years. From an even earlier age young people are assessed according to their suitability for divisions such as the paratroops, the air force or the infantry and tank corps. A career in the army is considered highly prestigious and it's a matter of considerable pride among many senior civilians that they once served as officers.

held in 2009, resulting in a coalition between the Kadima and Likud parties. **Binyamin Netanyahu**, leader of the right-wing Likud Party, is currently prime minister.

Although at the time of writing Israel is in a state of tentative peace, the status quo is threatened by the expiry in 2010 of a moratorium on construction by Israel on the West Bank. Furthermore, widespread anti-government protests throughout the Middle East in 2011 led to further destabilization of the entire region.

GOVERNMENT AND ECONOMY

Israel is a multiparty parliamentary democracy. The **Knesset** (parliament) of 120 members is elected by proportional representation from party lists, rather than individual candidates.

The new leader of the party or coalition that has the greatest chance of forming a government, usually with an absolute majority, is invited by the existing president to do so. The prime minister's election is slightly different, decided by separate universal vote. The president of state, meanwhile, is elected by the Knesset every five years by secret ballot. The presidency is the highest office in Israel and the president is considered to be above day-to-day politics, but he does appoint judges to the Supreme Court, which is the safeguard of the country's democracy. The **Supreme Court** has the authority to intervene at all levels of life in Israel, from politics to economic matters, and is held in enormous respect by the people. Israelis are obsessed with politics and lively political debate is part of everyday life, so be prepared to join in.

Israel has suffered from high **inflation** in the past, partly due to the cost of maintaining its defence force; proportionally the country has one of the highest defence budgets in the world.

The economy, which has moved from agricultural to post-industrial, is relatively stable now with steady growth, but life for the visitor is not cheap. Israel's main exports include computer software, military equipment, cut diamonds, chemicals and agricultural products. Roughly half of the government's external debt is owed to the USA, its major source of economic and military aid. The country's income includes US$2.4 billion from tourism generated by 2.3 million visitors.

THE PEOPLE

Below: *Ultra-Orthodox Jews devote their days to reading the Torah and praying.*

If there was ever a cultural melting pot, Israel is it. Under the **Law of Return**, any Jew, anywhere in the world, has the right to live in Israel and take Israeli citizenship. This is what has brought wave after wave of immigrants, from the first Russians who arrived in 1882 to Germans, North Africans and, later, an estimated one million Soviet Jews looking for a new life of freedom after many years under Communism.

Israel's population is around 7.47 million. **Tel Aviv** has a population of 390,000, the total of its metropolitan area extending to 3.3 million. **Jerusalem**, meanwhile, has 910,300 residents. Israel's third city is **Haifa**, on the coast, with a more mixed Arab and Jewish population and also the world centre of the Baha'i religion

More than four-fifths of the Israeli population is Jewish, with 1.15 million Muslims and the rest

Christians, Druze and others. While all these communities live and worship alongside one another, cultural boundaries remain clear and visitors will encounter second generation Armenians and Ethiopians who still speak as though they've just arrived in the country.

Native-born Israelis are nicknamed sabras, a cactus fruit which is tough and thorny on the outside and sweet on the inside. But in reality, Israelis are incredibly hospitable and naturally curious about visitors. Family ties are strong in Israel and in Jewish families Friday nights, the eve of the Sabbath, are spent at home. Children are welcomed everywhere and usually stay up quite late.

Israelis are not big drinkers. A more typical night out consists of drinking coffee and talking. Young people are surprisingly mature, thanks to their three years' compulsory national service (two for girls), and tend to be great travellers and lovers of the outdoors.

Israeli people in general are hard-working, aggressive in business and highly demonstrative: shouting and gesticulating doesn't necessarily mean anger but discussion. Israelis are also immersed in politics, which is discussed endlessly on the radio and TV and in the many daily newspapers. By all means enter into a political discussion, but remember to have your argument well prepared.

SAMARITANS

The handful of Samaritans left in Israel today are descended from those mentioned in the Bible. By the time the Jews returned from Babylon, the Samaritans, who had stayed, had inter-married with the invaders and, while they adhered to the Jewish faith, were not considered pure. Strong antipathy arose between the two groups. The holiest site for Samaritans today is Mount Gerizim, where they once had a temple, later destroyed by the Hasmoneans. During Samaritan Passover, lambs are sacrificed here, although non-Samaritan spectators are asked to leave for the ritual.

Language

The diversity of the population is reflected in the number of languages you'll hear on the streets: **Hebrew**, **Yiddish**, **English**, **German**, **Arabic**, **French**, **Spanish**, **Amharic** (spoken by Ethiopian Jews) and **Russian**. Israel Radio broadcasts in 12 different languages. Hebrew and Arabic, however, are the official languages, with English widely understood. Hebrew today is actually similar to biblical Hebrew, with an expanded vocabulary and a few English words thrown in. While the visitor can get by in virtually any language, it is only polite – and much appreciated by the locals – to learn a few words of Hebrew.

Few foreign-language television programmes are dubbed, so if you're learning Hebrew, watching TV is a perfect way to practise. Alternatively, there is plenty of choice in reading matter. Israel has 26 daily newspapers, more than any other country in the world, published in Hebrew, Arabic, Russian and English. For English-speaking visitors, *The Jerusalem Post* is a good, if rather right-wing read.

Religion

As well as forming the spiritual home of **Judaism**, Jerusalem in particular is the world's most important **Christian** site and is of great significance to **Muslims**. Israel is also home to **Samaritans**, **Armenians**, **Eastern Orthodox**, **Druze** and forms the world headquarters of the **Baha'i**. Freedom of worship is guaranteed and, whatever your faith, you will be welcome. Of Israel's seven million inhabitants, some 5.6 million are Jewish and only 20% of these claim to be 'practising' Jews, which means daily prayer, religious observance of the Sabbath and keeping a kosher household.

Shabbat (the Sabbath) – from sundown on Friday to sundown on Saturday – is a time of rest, contemplation and prayer and is strictly observed: exact times of sunset are published in the newspapers. Shops and restaurants close, offices are deserted, and public transport stops, except in Tel Aviv. In religious households, people don't cook or switch on any appliance, although nowadays electric timers are used to operate household lights and food is prepared the day before and kept warm.

On Friday nights, traditional Shabbat supper is served. At sunset on Saturday, a Havdalah candle is lit to mark the passing of the holy day and a blessing is read. The family drinks a glass of kosher wine and passes round a pot of sweet-smelling spices for everybody to inhale.

Shabbat need not affect the visitor. Many of the non-kosher restaurants stay open and there is plenty of activity in the big hotels. In Tel Aviv, after supper, huge crowds turn out to stroll along the promenade in the warm night air. Jerusalem is more observant and the streets are very quiet on a Friday night.

Men in long black coats and black hats, with distinctive locks of hair around their faces, belong to the ultra-Orthodox sect, the devout **Hassidic Jews** who still dress as their original Eastern European predecessors did 200 years ago. They live in ghettos, the largest of which is **Me'a She'arim** in Jerusalam, almost recreating the conditions of the Eastern Europe they left behind, with narrow alleys and high, forbidding walls. Many of them do not serve in the army – a source of great irritation to the Israelis – and furthermore, do not work, preferring to study the Scriptures instead.

Strangely, a number of Hassidic Jews do not even believe in the State of Israel. Their doctrine insists that the State of Israel will only exist after the coming of the Messiah, which they believe has not yet happened. Visitors to Me'a She'arim are politely warned at the entrance to dress with extreme modesty.

Above: *The Church of the Holy Sepulchre is the heart of Jerusalem's Christian Quarter.*

Festivals and Holidays
With so many different religions practised here, life in Israel seems like one long holiday. Christians observe Christmas and Easter, Muslims Ramadan, and Jews the 13 holidays on the Jewish Calendar, which are 'official' as far as shops and businesses are concerned. But Israelis will also celebrate New Year's Eve. The Hebrew calendar

THE SECT OF MYSTERY

The **Druze** are a mysterious sect of around 60,000 people, living in the mountains around Carmel, and are descended from an Egyptian religious movement of some 900 years ago. The men dress distinctively in a white headdress, black bloomers and cummerbund and they sport bushy moustaches. No-one knows exactly what Druze beliefs entail, as they have been kept a secret through the generations, although reincarnation does play a part. Despite their enigmatic air, Druze are successfully integrated into Israeli society and unlike some sects – the Hassidim, for example – they serve their time in the Israeli Defence Force.

Below: *Sukkot is also known as the Harvest Festival and is a time of great celebration.*

is based on the lunar year, so holiday dates do not follow the Gregorian calendar. God is said to have created the earth in 3760BC, which corresponds to the Gregorian year 0. Thus 2009 is the year 5769 and so on.

Rosh Hashanah and Yom Kippur

Jewish New Year – Rosh Hashanah – falls in September or October. As the only two-day public holiday, this is the time when urban-dwelling Israelis head for the beach, the Sea of Galilee or the mountains. For the religious, this is a time of self-examination. Ten days later is the **Day of Atonement**, or Yom Kippur, which is the holiest day of the year. Everything stops while the religious fast from sunset to sunset, and spend the day in the synagogue.

Sukkot and Simchat Torah

Sukkot, the **Harvest Festival**, is only a week or so after Yom Kippur. Every family builds a *succah*, a temporary shelter made of palm branches and leaves. Under its roof the family eats for seven days, commemorating the structures under which the Israelites lived during the exodus from Egypt. On the fifth day, there are parades and walks around Jerusalem. The last of the autumn vacations, the **Rejoicing of the Torah** (the first five books of the Bible), means singing and dancing in the streets with the Torah Scroll.

Hanukkah

The **Feast of Lights** in December celebrates the Jews recapturing their Holy Temple from the Greeks, who tried to suppress the Jewish faith. Hanukkah candles are lit on a menorah, the seven- or eight-branched candelabrum owned by every

household. Small jelly-filled doughnuts
are eaten everywhere, and children enjoy
parties and games.

Passover

Passover, or **Pesach**, in March or April,
celebrates the liberation of the ancient
Israelites from Egypt. No bread or yeast
is eaten for a week – just unleavened
matzos – and people rid their houses of
anything containing yeast, an excuse for
a good spring-cleaning. The Passover
dinner, or Seder, is a feast symbolizing
the experiences of the Israelites as they
fled from Egypt, including bitter herbs
representing the bitterness of slavery.

Above: *Lighting the
menorah is a ritual of
Hanukkah.*

Traditional Cultures

Dance, art and theatre are prolific in Israel and there
are cultural performances everywhere, from the smallest kibbutz to the theatre stages of Jerusalem and Tel
Aviv. As well as classical ballet, dance incorporates
several ethnic styles, such as Hassidic, Arabic and
Yemenite folk dancing. There are many dance companies, from big international groups like **Batsheva** to
the **Kibbutz Contemporary Dance Company** and any
number of smaller fringe groups. Tel Aviv and Jerusalem both have a lively theatre and dance scene.

The Arts

Israel's magnificent landscapes have inspired countless
painters and there are large artistic communities in
Jaffa, the village of Ein Hod near Haifa, and Safed in
the Galilee region. Important galleries include the
Israel Museum in Jerusalem, which houses works of
contemporary Israeli art, Jewish European art and sculpture, a vast number of European works and a modern
section. In Tel Aviv, don't miss the **Helena Rubenstein
Pavillion**, the collections of which include European
and American art from the 17th to the 20th centuries,

PUBLIC HOLIDAYS AND FESTIVALS

The official holidays are
Jewish holidays and Shabbat,
but each religion has the
right to observe its own
holidays. Public holidays
and Shabbat take place from
sunset to sunset. The main
Jewish holidays are listed in
the panel on page 19.

or the wonderful **Tel Aviv Museum of Art**, with a fantastic contemporary collection.

The **Israel Philharmonic Orchestra** is world famous and often features well-known guest performers. The orchestra's home is the **Mann Auditorium** in Tel Aviv and tickets are usually hard to come by. In Jerusalem, try to see the **Jerusalem Symphony Orchestra**, which performs weekly throughout the winter. Its home is the Henry Crown Hall at the beautiful **Jerusalem Centre for the Performing Arts**.

There are numerous theatre groups in Tel Aviv and Jerusalem, although if you're travelling around, nothing quite beats the romance of theatre at dusk in the beautiful Roman amphitheatre at **Caesarea**, 50km (31 miles) from Tel Aviv, as the sun sets across the waves. There are theatre performances here as well as an annual jazz festival. In Tel Aviv, the **Habima Theatre** is the home of the National Theatre of Israel, while performances are also staged at the **Suzanne Dellal Centre for Dance and Theatre** at Neve Tzedek. The city's flagship venue, though, is the **Tel Aviv Performing Arts Centre**, home to the famous Israeli Opera.

Jerusalem has several theatres, the main one being the **Jerusalem Centre for the Performing Arts**.

Nightlife

Tel Aviv has the liveliest nightlife, with a cutting-edge lounge bar and club scene to rival Ibiza or Ayia Napa, only cooler. The **New Port** and **Lilienblum Street** are the hottest spots for nightlife. Pop concerts are held in Tel Aviv's Ha-Yarkon Park, under the stars. Jerusalem is less

---

FABULOUS FESTIVALS

Not to be confused with religious holidays, there are numerous colourful cultural festivals in the Israeli calendar.
March: Tel Aviv Classical Music Festival.
April: Independence Day Gala Concert.
May: Israel Festival of Music and Dance in Tel Aviv and Jerusalem.
June: Israeli Opera Festival, Masada, and Jerusalem Light Festival.
July: International Film Festival.
August: International Street Theatre Festival, Bat Yam.
October: Suzanne Dellal International Dance Competition, Tel Aviv.
December: Choir Festival, Jerusalem.

exciting for clubbing but has a lively café society and a growing bar scene in the side streets off the **Jaffa Road**.

Sport in Israel

Israelis are generally active, outdoor types and there are countless opportunities to indulge in sports, from the everyday to the extreme, although with the exception of **cycling** and **beach sports**, most of the following activities require a trip out of the city. Israel is so small that this is not difficult to arrange.

Hiking is very popular, some of the best areas being the Negev Desert and the Galilee region. In the Negev (reachable from Jerusalem for a short break or a long day), there are marked trails in the national parks like Ein Gedi, overlooking the Dead Sea, although many locals prefer to hike away from the tourist areas, camping out overnight. **Mountain biking**, **rappelling** and **off-road driving** are all popular in this area, too.

A visit to Eilat is an ideal opportunity to try **scuba diving** in the Red Sea's warm, clear waters with their spectacular coral reefs. A starter course takes just one day. For those who prefer not to dive, the **snorkelling** is almost as good. On the Mediterranean coast, meanwhile, **sea kayaking** and **sailing** are popular sports.

In Tel Aviv, hire a bike and cycle along the beachfront, or jog in the early morning. Locals are keen runners and there's an annual half marathon and marathon. **Surfing** is excellent here, with international competitions during summer. **Sailing** is popular, too. Everybody plays beach games, including *matkot*, a national institution, with bats and a ping pong ball, Frisbee and volleyball.

Opposite: *The Suzanne Dellal Centre is one of the top performing arts venues in Tel Aviv.* **Below:** *A windsurfer catches a strong breeze off one of Tel Aviv's magnificent beaches.*

FESTIVAL NOSH

On Hanukkah, small jelly doughnuts, or *sufganiot*, are eaten throughout Israel, as well as *latkes*, or potato pancakes. In January or February on Tu B'Shevat or Arbour Day, families eat fruit from biblical times such as olives, dates, pomegranates and figs. During Passover, everybody eats unleavened bread, in the form of wafers made of specially dried flour. The tradition stems from when Moses and the Israelites fled from Egypt – there was no time to leave bread to rise, so they ate flat loaves. Tastier Passover fare includes coconut macaroons. If you dine with Jewish families on Shabbat, expect *cholent*, a bean and meat stew that is baked on Friday.

Below: *Israelis love to eat on the go and bagels are a popular fast food.*

Food and Drink

A biblical law that 'a kid shall not seethe in its mother's milk' led to the rule that meat and milk should not be mixed. A **kosher** restaurant or home will keep two sets of crockery and utensils, one for milk and one for meat. Scavenging creatures like pigs and shellfish are considered unclean and are not eaten, although all sorts of crafty imitations do appear, like 'prawns' and crabsticks made of fish. Many Jews (Orthodox) will eat vegetarian food in a restaurant where the kosher observance is slightly suspect.

Coming to terms with all the complexities of kosher and non-kosher takes a while but most visitors are amazed at the variety they find in Israel's cuisine: a breakfast buffet groaning under cheese platters and mounds of fruit or a candlelit feast of Chateaubriand washed down with a very palatable local red wine.

Many restaurants and most hotels observe Jewish law, selling either meat or dairy products, but never both. A meat restaurant will serve margarine – not butter – non-dairy cream and no cheese sauces.

Vegetarians will love the dairy restaurants, which are great for pasta, delicious cheeses, salad bars and creamy desserts. Most hotels have at least one outlet of each type.

'Typical' Israeli cuisine does not really exist. Like the people, Israeli food is a **collection of cultures**, with Mediterranean, Lebanese and other Middle Eastern influences. Tel Aviv in particular has a thriving restaurant scene, with some of the finest establishments in the Mediterranean region. If anything does typify eating in Israel, it's the simple dishes from the Middle East region, which include falafel – tiny balls of lentils, deep fried and stuffed into pitta bread – with salad; hummus, a garlicky chick-pea dip; and smooth tahini, a

paste made of sesame seeds. Kebabs of veal, chicken, lamb or beef are sold everywhere, usually with a vast salad. Try the *harit*, a spicy condiment that peps up the blandest falafel. Eastern European cooking, often regarded (wrongly) as 'typical' Jewish food, features in some homes: dishes include gefilte fish, chopped liver, borscht and Hungarian goulash.

Above: *Falafel are the staple diet of Israelis, served with pitta, hummus and salad.*

Fish is sold everywhere. Grilled sardines are served on the beaches, and fishermen in Galilee still bring in plump freshwater trout and the tasty St Peter fish, as they did in biblical times, which are sold in the swish restaurants of Tel Aviv and Jerusalem.

Of course, not all restaurants are kosher. An influx of Chinese, Vietnamese and Filipinos has led to the establishment of many **Asian** restaurants, with pork and prawns in abundance. Israel has its fair share of **fast-food** outlets, too, particularly in the big cities, although most Israelis would always opt for a good falafel rather than McDonald's.

Fruit in Israel is magnificent and the markets have spectacular fruit displays. Kiwi, mango, pomegranate, passion fruit, custard apple and papaya are grown here, as are the world's largest strawberries and endless varieties of citrus.

Fruit juices from street vendors are wonderfully refreshing. **Coffee** is served black, strong and sweet (Turkish) or creamy and frothy (Viennese). *Botz* is the strong Israeli version of Turkish coffee.

Israelis are not big drinkers but the country produces some good **wines** (red and white) from the Carmel region, the Galilee and Rishon le-Zion, southeast of Tel Aviv. Local **beers**, bottled and draft, are available, and the local aniseed-flavoured firewater is called arak.

KEEPING IT KOSHER

'Kosher' comes from the Hebrew *kasher*, meaning 'fit' or 'proper'. It is applied especially to the food that Jews are permitted to eat. According to the Bible only animals that have cloven hooves and are ruminant (that is, chew the cud) are considered kosher. These animals must be killed according to the traditional rabbinical ritual and soaked, salted, and washed to remove any traces of blood. Milk or milk products must not be eaten with meat, and shellfish is prohibited. During the Passover Festival, only unleavened bread is to be eaten.

2
Old Jaffa and Neve Tzedek

Against the setting of biblical landscapes that have served as a backdrop to 5000 years of history, Tel Aviv is incongruously young, having celebrated its 100th birthday with a year-long party in 2009. But it's true: Israel's biggest beach resort, home to some three million people, is a very recent phenomenon. Not that it's one you could easily forget, with its miles of sandy beaches, its skyscrapers glittering in the hot Mediterranean sun and its hopping nightlife. There's a lot of truth in the popular Israeli saying that 'Jerusalem prays, Haifa pays and Tel Aviv plays'.

Yet there's a lot more to Tel Aviv than beaches and nightclubs. The city's eclectic architectural style reflects the aspirations of the many new waves of immigrants back in the early 20th century: their dreams of re-creating the neoclassical grace of Vienna, ornate experimentation with **Art Nouveau** and the minimalist lines of **Bauhaus** style. Against this setting, futuristic glass skyscrapers have shot up in the 21st century, while the crumbling mansions of **Neve Tzedek**, one of the earliest 20th-century suburbs on the city's southern fringes, newly restored, now command the highest real estate prices in Israel.

Tel Aviv leads the way in Israel's cuisine, fashion and the arts, with some of the finest restaurants in the Mediterranean on offer. Up-and-coming designers showcase their wares in formerly shabby but suddenly chic neighbourhoods, while the city is the country's focal point of theatre, classical music and ballet.

DON'T MISS

*** **Old Jaffa:** free walking tours on Wednesdays.
*** **Ilana Goor Museum:** a fascinating example of living with art.
*** **Dr Shakshuka:** go for lunch in Jaffa Flea Market.
*** **Neve Tzedek:** wander from bar to bar in this trendy district.
*** Enjoy a day out on the **beach**.

Opposite: *Old Jaffa Port has recently undergone a massive renovation.*

All this is overlooked by ancient **Jaffa**, clinging to a rocky outcrop to the south of Tel Aviv's beaches, a solid reminder that life was going on here several thousand years before the current technological age – indeed, before the Crusades and even before Christ. Jaffa today is beautifully preserved, its tangle of stone alleyways the haunt of artists and sculptors, its mainly Arab population living peacefully side by side with its brash, flashy, multicultural neighbour.

OLD JAFFA ★★★

Jaffa, or **Yafo**, as it's known locally, is one of the oldest cities in the world. Although layer upon layer has been added over centuries, the site on which Old Jaffa sits has produced relics from as long ago as the 18th century BC.

Today, it's a cluster of winding, pedestrianized streets and ancient houses, clinging to a rocky hill on the waterfront south of Tel Aviv, still crammed into its for-

tified walls. The community, a mixture of Jews, Muslims and Christians, secular and religious, lives peacefully in close quarters, a mixture of the artistic, the young and funky, the elderly, who have spent their lives here, and the usual array of immigrants you'd expect in any part of Israel. By day, the streets are buzzing with tourists shopping for art and enjoying some of the city's most celebrated restaurants and patisseries (don't miss lunch on the hoof from **Abouelafia**, Jaffa's famous 24-hour bakery on Yefet Street), as well as visiting the famous flea market. At night, the church, fortifications and ancient lighthouse are floodlit, creating an image dear to the hearts of residents of Tel Aviv.

Getting orientated is easy. Busy **Yefet Street** bisects the area; its start is marked by the **Clock Tower**. On its other side is the **Flea Market**. Every week, the Association for tourism Tel Aviv-Jaffa offers tourists four free English-guided tours, with no advance reser-

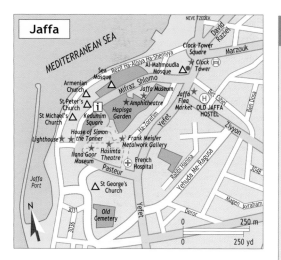

Jaffa

FIRST PRIME MINISTER OF ISRAEL

David Ben-Gurion (1886–1973) dedicated his life to establishing a Jewish homeland in Palestine. He left his native Poland in 1906 to work on a farm in a Jewish settlement in Turkish Palestine. In 1910 he became editor of the Zionist workers' newspaper, *Achdut*. In 1940 he formed the Mapai, the Zionist labour party. Throughout World War II, Ben-Gurion battled to allow Jews to immigrate to Palestine and he became the first prime minister of the new Israel. He remained in the Knesset until his retirement from politics in 1970. For the last 10 years of his life he lived at Sede Boqer, a kibbutz in the Negev. He died there in 1973.

vation required: Art and architecture at Tel Aviv University (Mondays at 11:00); Old Jaffa (Wednesdays at 09:30); Tel Aviv by night (Tuesdays at 20:00); and Bauhaus Tel Aviv (Saturdays at 11:00).

Jaffa Visitors' Centre ★
There's a small, subterranean visitors' centre at the entrance to the old town on **Kedumim Square**, mainly underground, showing relics from Jaffa's long history and an audiovisual presentation (in English and other languages) about the port's past. Open daily 10:00–18:00.

The Clock Tower ★
The **Ottoman Clock Tower**, dating back to 1906, was built on Yefet Street in the Ottoman era to commemorate Sultan Abdul Hamid the Second's 25th year in power. At the heart of Jaffa, the clock is the city's meeting place, as well as the starting point for the free guided tours offered by the tourist board. A series of stained-glass windows around the tower tells the story of the town's history. The courtyard opposite was once an **Armenian hostel**, a kind of staging post for travellers going to and from the Jewish settlements inland.

Opposite: *Jaffa's Clock Tower is a focal point of the old town and the meeting place for the free weekly guided walking tours.*

FOUNDING FATHERS

Tel Aviv is actually the first Jewish city to have been built in 2000 years. In 1909, a group of 66 families from the overcrowded, predominantly Arab port of Jaffa staked their claim on the sand dunes to the north. They drew lines in the sand and then divided up the imaginary plots by holding a lottery using sea shells. The new suburb which they created – named Tel Aviv, or Hill of Spring – expanded rapidly until, in 1948, it became the de facto capital of Israel (the Israelis consider Jerusalem as the capital but the UN doesn't and many embassies are located in Tel Aviv). The city celebrated its 100th birthday in 2009 with festivals, parades, musical performances and a touring 'Tel Aviv Beach' that was set up in Paris, Vienna and New York's Central Park.

BOTZ, THE BUTCH DRINK

Botz, which means 'mud' in Hebrew, is a very macho kind of coffee drink in Israel. Like Turkish coffee, it's very strong and drunk black. Unlike Turkish coffee, in which the sludge is left at the bottom of the cup, the *botz* drinker swallows the grounds (the coffee is stirred so the solids float around). If this prospect is too awful, then ask for 'Nes' which is ordinary Nescafé, or a 'café afooch' (guttural ch) which is like a cappuccino.

Further along the road, past the police station, is the **Al-Mahamoudia Mosque**, built in 1812 and named after the then Turkish governor. Non-Muslims are not allowed inside. **Jaffa Museum** is located in the former **City Hall**, which has also served as a post office, public bath and police station.

St Peter's Church ★

The imposing St Peter's Church was built by Franciscan monks between 1888 and 1894. There has been a church on the site, close to where St Peter is said to have had a visitation from an angel, for centuries, once serving as a hostel for pilgrims on their way to Jerusalem. There was also a Crusader castle here. Down a narrow alley close by is the **House of Simon the Tanner**, who is mentioned in the Bible (Acts 10:9–47) and who was playing host to Peter at the time of the visitation. The house is inhabited today by an Armenian family and is not open to the public, although its ancient façade still attracts a stream of visitors. The family was once responsible for operating Jaffa's iconic **lighthouse**, a city landmark, although this is done automatically now.

Shopping and Galleries in Old Jaffa ★★★

Lose yourself in the old streets of the city's heart, which are pedestrianized. You'll find quaint little jewellery shops, galleries, cafés and artists' studios in the tangle of alleys named after signs of the zodiac.

Some of Tel Aviv's top artists are based in Jaffa, where you have to be successful in order to afford the rent. **Frank Meisler**'s amazing metalwork **gallery** is definitely worth a visit; Margaret Thatcher, Prince Charles and the Duchess of Cornwall are all owners of the **Jerusalem Globe**, a gold and silver orb, the top half of which forms an intricate 3D model of the city's skyline.

Call in at the **Hasimta Theatre**, Tel Aviv-Jaffa's most famous fringe theatre, with a wonderful rooftop bar that hosts a jazz evening on Wednesdays at 21:30.

Look out, too, for **Adina Plastelina**. Adina is a young, funky jewellery designer making items out of brightly coloured plastic dough which is rolled in layers into intricate sausages, each one with an image at the centre, and sliced vertically to create pretty earrings, rings and brooches. What's interesting about her atelier is that it's a 3500-year-old Turkish bath and she and her partner, Sima, have maintained the building with many of its original features, displaying bits of pottery dating back to 1500BC.

Above: *The fascinating Ilana Goor Museum in Old Jaffa, one of many art galleries to explore.*

Ilana Goor Museum ★★★
This fascinating museum on Mazal Dagim Street in Old Jaffa is an example of living with art. A hostel for Jewish pilgrims in the 18th century, today it is the home of artist and sculptor **Ilana Goor**, who opens most of her personal living space to the public. There are spectacular sculptures, many using agricultural tools; whole rooms containing just one scene, often of strange metal birds and insects; and some beautiful paintings, as well as the artist's personal collection of paintings, carvings, castings and etchings from her travels worldwide. There's a sculpture garden on the roof with wonderful views of the port and coastline, a great place to sit quietly with a drink after a visit. Open 10:00–16:00 Sun–Fri and 10:00–18:00 Sat.

Jaffa Flea Market ★★
The famous flea market is opposite Old Jaffa, across Yefet Street, from Sunday to Friday. It's a treasure trove of junk (and the occasional find) spilling out of the buildings and warehouses, offering anything from oriental rugs to knock-off designer jeans. The market was established in the 19th century and has changed little since.

Thursdays in July and August are great days to visit as it stays open late and there are all sorts of additional stalls, street performers and open-air displays, giving the place even more of a party feel. Open Sunday–Thursday, 09:00–17:00 (later in summer); Fri 09:00–14:00.

Hapisga Garden ★

Between Old Jaffa and the Clock Tower, this tranquil green space is a grassy mound with amazing views northwards along the coast to the towers of **Tel Aviv**. It's accessed by the **Bridge of Dreams**, a wooden footbridge adorned with beautiful bronze plaques of zodiac signs by local designers Esther Shlomo and Freddy Fabian. Legend has it that if you stand by your sign and gaze out to sea, your wish will come true.

Port of Jaffa ★

The port, one of the oldest documented in the world, recently underwent a massive renovation, partly for the Tel Aviv/Jaffa Centenary that took place in 2009 and partly because it had become somewhat run down. A new yacht marina, shops, galleries and restaurants are all being developed. Meanwhile, you can still visit the **Nalaga'at** (Please Touch) Centre, a cultural and entertainment complex run by deaf and blind people. There's a theatre, a café and a restaurant where diners eat in darkness to give them an idea of what it's like to be blind.

Neve Tzedek ★★★

Neve Tzedek was one of the first areas of what's now Tel Aviv to spring up in 1880, when Jaffa had by far exceeded its capacity and needed to expand beyond the walls. At this time, the land outside the walls was just rolling sand dunes and fruit orchards, along a vast beach that extended for miles to the north. Fine mansions were built amidst the orchards and over the years Neve Tzedek became a centre for literature and art. The suburb preceded modern Tel Aviv, which wasn't started until 1909.

Although the new community prospered, Neve Tzedek fell into disrepair during the second half of the 20th century when Tel Aviv's residents, with a taste for the new and shiny, began to be attracted to the even more contemporary areas closer to the city centre. As often happens, though, the area's fortunes reversed when young people began to return to the suburb, renovating the lovely old villas and in the process pushing prices sky-high.

Moving into Neve Tzedek nowadays requires an enormous budget, but even those who can't afford to live there visit for the bars, restaurants, culture and museums. In the narrow streets of the neighbourhood, you'll find achingly hip cafés and bars alongside avant-garde jewellery shops.

Nachum Gutman Museum ★

This permanent exhibition in an old mansion on Neve Tzedek Street commemorates the life and work of one of Israel's most famous artists and children's book illustrators, **Nachum Gutman**. The museum was established in May 1998 in the **Writers' House**, a building famed for its literary inhabitants and resident intellectuals between 1907 and 1914. Today, it houses permanent and temporary art exhibitions, the most popular being the brightly coloured and often whimsical work of Gutman himself, with whose work every Israeli child grows up. Gutman documents through his art the development of Tel Aviv in the early days and a visit here is a fascinating insight into the city's growth. It is open 10:00–16:00 Sunday–Thursday; 10:00–14:00 Friday; and 10:00–15:00 Saturday.

> ### JAFFA ORANGES
>
> The Jaffa orange, also known as the Shamouti orange, is a very sweet, almost seedless fruit. It is oval in shape and has a sweet flavour and pale-coloured peel.
>
> The oranges were grown around Jaffa long before the creation of the State of Israel and, at the height of their popularity, thousands of cases were being shipped to the UK. Nowadays, however, they have been replaced in Europe by oranges grown in the EU, which undercut Israel's produce in price. Furthermore, citrus fruits consume a lot of water and because of constant shortages in Israel, the citrus business is in decline. Jaffa oranges will always, however, be immortalized in one of Britain's favourite cookies, the orange-and-chocolate Jaffa Cake.

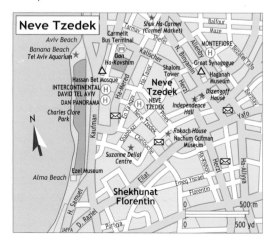

Above: *This colourful mural in Neve Tzedek depicts the history of this desirable, bohemian neighbourhood.*

JAFFA IN THE BIBLE

Jaffa is one of the oldest towns in Israel, believed to have been founded some 5000 years ago by **Japeth**, son of Noah. The town appears in the Bible in various places. It was the point at which cedars of Lebanon (sent from King Hiriam of Tyre for use in Solomon's Temple) were unloaded, and the departure point of Jonah on his legendary voyage to Tarshish, on which he was swallowed by a whale and regurgitated three days later. There's a whale statue in the city today, commemorating the Bible story.

Rokach House ★★

Lea Majaro-Mintz, a sculptor and also the granddaughter of the original owner of this beautiful villa on Simon Rokach Street, was one of the main influences of the revival of Neve Tzedek. She wanted to restore the house but she was denied permission, so she sued the city and won, inspiring the then mayor to put more resources into the area. Today, the house is both a museum and a performance venue, recreating the Tel Aviv of 100 years ago, with family relics and places like the kitchen preserved exactly as they were. There are plays and readings in the evenings (in Hebrew) and guests are served Jewish food based on 100-year-old recipes. The evenings are not so relevant if you don't understand Hebrew but the house itself is fascinating, not least for the hundreds of Majaro-Mintz's partly comical, partly depressing little clay sculptures of oppressed women in various poses. It is open Friday and Saturday only, 10:00–14:00.

Suzanne Dellal Centre

The Suzanne Dellal Centre is a well-known performing arts venue at the heart of Neve Tzedek, an attractive plaza at its centre, lined with outdoor cafés and restaurants. The building is on the site of two old schools that developed with the very beginnings of Tel Aviv, and in 1989 were converted into an artistic and cultural complex. Today, the centre is the home of the **Batsheva Dance Company**, the **Neve Tzedek Theatre** and the **Inbal Dance Company**. It's a wonderful place to come for a performance on a summer's evening. Start with drinks in the piazza and, after the show, move on to one of the many restaurants in the neighbourhood and then to the clubs and lounge bars nearby.

Nina Café, which doubles up as a small all-suite hotel, is a great place for a drink, especially in the pretty garden, while **Jajo Vino** is one of the area's hippest bars. **Nana Bar**, with its exposed brickwork and smooth wooden bar, is packed on a Friday night with the city's coolest people.

Jaffa and Neve Tzedek Beaches ★★★

Although it's hard to tell where one beach ends and another begins, there are distinctions, namely whether you have to pay, what's on offer and what kind of crowd favours which beach. But a trip to Tel Aviv is not complete without a day on the beach, or a moonlit stroll, or an early morning run.

Alma Beach

This is the stretch of sand where Tel Aviv ends and Jaffa begins, with lovely views of Old Jaffa. There's no life-guard here and no breakwaters, so you'll see a lot of surfers – but take care swimming as the waves can be huge. This is a peaceful beach, though, and location of the up-market fish restaurant **Manta Ray**, which also has a lounge area with big, squashy mattresses where you can lie back with a cocktail and watch the sunset.

Dolphinarium Beach/Banana Beach

Close to the end of the walkable strip between Tel Aviv and Jaffa, this expanse of sand – known as Dolphin-arium Beach, merging into the hip Banana Beach – ends in a breakwater and a jumble of rocks, on top of which sits the derelict old Dolphinarium.

There's nothing special on the beach here but on Friday nights you can stroll down at sunset and clamber up the rocks to listen to the hippie drummers. It's a free-for-all session of **bongos** and any other kind of drum, with dancing, drinking beer from a scruffy shack and an amazing energy.

PLANT A TREE FOR ISRAEL

Israelis plant trees for birth-days and weddings. Six million trees have been planted some 20km (12 miles) from Jerusalem in honour of the Jews who died in the Holocaust. For visitors, the **Holy Land Foundation** co-ordinates tree planting in six areas of Israel. For a nominal fee, you may plant a tree and receive a certificate, a copy of the Planter's Prayer and a lapel pin. The **Jewish National Fund** (JNF), meanwhile, has planted over 240 million trees over the last century for weddings, bar mitzvahs and birthdays (see www.jnf.org).

BEACH ETIQUETTE

• Beaches are safe and crime-free day and night, one of the great joys of Tel Aviv.
• Sunbathing months are April to October but people walk, jog, cycle and surf on the beach year-round.
• Watch out for dog mess – the Israelis aren't great at cleaning up!
• Swim near the lifeguard stations – the sea can be rough. Don't swim when the black flag is flying.
• Watch out for the strength of the sun. The cooling sea breeze can be deceptive.
• Big storms can wash up huge jellyfish, which can sting even when dead. If you're surfing, you might want to wear a wetsuit.

Old Jaffa and Neve Tzedek at a Glance

BEST TIMES TO VISIT

Tel Aviv is a year-round city but if you want to sit on the beach, March to October is best. Avoid July and August as it can get very humid. September is the period of a lot of the main Jewish holidays, so museums and attractions may be closed at odd hours.

GETTING THERE

Ben Gurion International, Israel's main airport, is situated 20km (12.5 miles) from the city, served by buses, trains and taxis. There's a small domestic airport, **Sde Dov**, north of the city, with flights to other parts of Israel. **Buses** in Tel Aviv are run by Dan, tel: 03 639 4444, www.dan.co.il and Egged, tel: 03 694 8888, www.egged.co.il Israel Railways operates frequent **trains** from the airport to three stops in Tel Aviv, tel: 03 611 7000, www.rail.co.il **Taxis** wait at the airport and operate on a meter.

GETTING AROUND

Tel Aviv has an efficient **bus** service, run mainly by Dan (see above) and with some Egged buses (see above). **Taxis** are inexpensive and can be hailed on the street. **Walking** is pleasant outside the main summer season; you can walk all the way from north Tel Aviv to Jaffa on the beach. It's not worth hiring a **car** unless you plan to leave

the city and need transport for day trips. **Car Rental:** Avis, 13 Ha-Yarkon St, tel: 1 700 700 222; Budget, 99 Ha-Yarkon St, tel: 1 700 704 141. Be green and hire a **bicycle** instead: tel: 03 544 2292, www.rentabike israel.com

WHERE TO STAY

All the big hotels are located along the beach. There isn't much accommodation in Jaffa and Neve Tzedek as there isn't much space, but you will find some wonderful smaller boutique hotels in this area and a couple of bigger hotels at the southern end of the beach promenade.

LUXURY

InterContinental David Tel Aviv, 12 Kaufman St, tel: 03 795 1111, www.ichotels group.com City landmark, five-star de luxe hotel on the southern end of the beach promenade, near Old Jaffa.
Dan Panorama, 10 Kaufman St, tel: 03 519 0190, www.danhotels.com Prominent tower block overlooking Old Jaffa, well located right by the beach promenade.
Nina Café Hotel, 29 Shabazi St, Neve Tzedek, tel: 03 510 5239, www.ninacafehotel. com Gorgeous boutique hotel with just nine beautiful suites attached to one of the trendiest bars, Nina Café, in the style of a Parisian coffee house.

MID-RANGE

Neve Tzedek Hotel, 4 Degania street, Neve Tzedek, tel: 054 207 0706, www.nevetzedekhotel.com This is a new boutique hotel from the owner of the legendary Nana Bar. It consists of just five suites, each with its own home cinema, Jacuzzi and garden or roof terrace.
Andromeda Hill Hotel, 3 Louis Pasteur St, Jaffa, tel: 03 683 8448, www.andromeda. co.il Luxurious self-catering apartments in a fantastic location in Jaffa. Residents have the use of a pool and a spa.

BUDGET

Old Jaffa Hostel, 13 Amiad Street, tel: 03 682 2370, www.telaviv-hostel.com Friendly hostel in a converted Turkish house, in the middle of the Jaffa flea market. Roof garden overlooking the sea.

WHERE TO EAT

Abouelafia, Yefet Street. A 24-hour take-away bakery on the main street, serving absolutely everything – falafel, wonderful cakes, slices of pizza, pies, pastries dripping with honey. It's a Jaffa institution.
Il Yaffo Caffè, by Jaffa Flea Market, tel: 03 518 1988, www.yaffocaffe.com Hugely popular café with stark, industrial design and curious flock wallpaper. Very hip. Don't miss the fabulous

Old Jaffa and Neve Tzedek at a Glance

ice creams – lemon mint, coffee meringue and chocolate orange are just three flavours on offer.

Nana Bar, 1 Ahad Haam St, Neve Tzedek, tel: 03 516 1915. This ultra-chic bar/ Parisian café is located in trendy Neve Tzedek.

Manta Ray, southern promenade, tel: 03 517 4773. A stylish and fashionable establishment, well situated right on the beach, serving superb fish dishes and Israeli salads.

Catit, 4 Heichal Ha-Talmud St, Neve Tzedek, tel: 03 510 7001. Chic restaurant in beautifully restored old mansion. This is a good place for power lunches and romantic dinners. Serves Mediterranean specialities.

Blackout, Nalaga'at Centre, Jaffa Port, tel: 03 633 0808. Kosher restaurant in Jaffa Port run by blind, deaf and dumb people (the name of the restaurant means 'please touch'), where you can enjoy the unusual experience of dining in the dark.

Dr Shakshuka, 3 Beit Eshel, Jaffa, tel: 03 682 2842. A local institution, filling a large courtyard by the flea market and packed at lunchtimes on market days. Try the *shakshuka* – egg baked in a spicy tomato sauce – as well as couscous, dips and salads, stews and hearty soups.

Cordelia Restaurant, Hazchuhit Street 1, Nir Zook Plaze, 68039 Tel Aviv-Yafo,

tel: 03 518 4668, www. cordelia.co.il This restaurant is owned and run by Nir Zook, Israel's celebrity chef. It is attached to the Jaffa Bar and the Bistro, forming a corridor between two buildings, with industrial, eclectic design. French and Middle Eastern specialities are served.

Yoezer Wine Bar, 2 Ish-Habira St, Jaffa, tel: 03 683 9115. An atmospheric wine bar/restaurant in an ancient building with vaulted ceiling. Hundreds of wines are sold by the glass in a chic setting, surrounded by huge flower arrangements. Friday and Saturday brunch are recommended in particular.

SHOPPING

Old Jaffa is a dream for artlovers, although it's not cheap. Keep hunting the narrow streets and tiny galleries for what you want and don't forget the museum shops – Ilana Goor's gift shop is fantastic. For designer fashion and gorgeous jewellery and accessories, wander the streets of Neve Tzedek. Jaffa Flea Market is a typical flea market, selling everything under the sun, including a lot of junk, but you may pick up a bargain there.

TOURS AND EXCURSIONS

Free guided walking tours of Jaffa (in English) take place on Wednesdays at 09:30 (except holidays). Groups meet at the Clock Tower. The Visitors' Centre also operates

a tourist information desk run by the **Old Jaffa Development Corporation** (tel: 03 518 4015), which offers a range of guided tours as well as additional attractions to visitors.

Visit the main **Tel Aviv tourist office** (*see* Useful Contacts below) and pick up a map of Neve Tzedek; there's a very good one showing enormous detail, so much so that you can do your own tour if that's what you'd prefer. Alternatively, you can hire a private guide; there's a list on www.goisrael.com

Take a **city tour** in an open-top bus, calling at all the main sights, including Old Jaffa. Visit http://city-tour.co.il for details.

USEFUL CONTACTS

Ben Gurion International Airport: flight information, tel: 03 972 3344.

Tourist Information Offices: Ben Gurion Airport, tel: 03 975 4260; 46 Herbert Samuel St, tel: 03 516 6188.

Tel Aviv-Jaffa Municipality, Yitzhak Rabin Square, tel: 03 521 8438. Also look out for the new mobile tourist information booth – a Segway, which tours the popular sites dispensing help and information.

Local information, visit www.visit-tlv.com

Police, tel: 100.

Magen David Adom First Aid, tel: 101.

Fire Department, tel: 102.

3
Central Tel Aviv

Not unlike New York, Tel Aviv is a series of neighbourhoods rather than one homogenous sprawl, and nowhere is this more apparent than the stretch between the ancient **Yemenite Quarter** in the south and the City Hall, overlooking the ceremonial **Yitzhak Rabin Square**. This compact area couldn't be more diverse if it tried, from the colourful hubbub of **Carmel Market** to the shabby chic of **Gan Ha-Hashmal**, the up-and-coming fashion district, to the beautiful **Rothschild Boulevard** and its neatly laid-out grid of gorgeous 1930s villas, most of them designed in the Bauhaus style.

Although Tel Aviv is the business and financial capital of Israel, there's a permanent holiday feel about it. Locals sip coffee or snack on sushi at trendy little booths along the tree-lined centre of Rothschild Boulevard, or they go jogging on the vast, sandy beaches before work in the morning, inhaling the fresh, salty air. Carmel Market is a daily riot of sounds, smells and colours, street stalls piled high with the amazing variety of fruit and vegetables that give Israelis their lean, healthy look. At weekends, Friday and Saturday in this part of the world, the street cafés are packed by day as everybody turns out for one of those famed Israeli breakfasts (*see* panel, page 47), and the clubs along **Lilienblum Street** throb late into the night.

Hundreds of restaurants are waiting to be discovered, many of them set in romantic old mansions, beautifully refurbished, diners feasting on fresh fish by candlelight in vine-covered gardens. And then there are

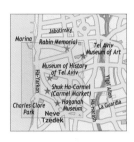

DON'T MISS

★★★ Take a walk through the **White City**.
★★★ Spend a Friday morning at **Carmel Market**.
★★ Shopping is excellent on **Sheinkin Street**.
★★ **Yeminite Vineyard:** for Yemenite specialities.
★★ **Beach life:** ball games, surfing, swimming and movies under the stars.

Opposite: *The modern towers of Tel Aviv from a vantage point in Old Jaffa.*

TOWN PLANNER EXTRAORDINAIRE

Scotsman Patrick Geddes (1854–1932) has become known as 'the father of town planning' and is responsible for the bright, airy layout and green spaces of modern Tel Aviv. He worked in many fields, including biology, botany and sociology, before moving on to town planning, with influences in Dundee, London, Paris and Tel Aviv, as well as Cyprus, America and Mexico. In India, Geddes produced community development schemes in and around Conjeevaram, Lahore, Lucknow, Nagpur and Pinjaur before being appointed the first Professor of Civics and Sociology at Bombay University. He died in Montpellier in 1932.

the beaches. Family beaches, surfers' beaches, beaches for posing, beaches for meditating on. All of them spotless, pounded by foaming rollers calmed by the many breakwaters, and all of them accessible, day or night. Tel Aviv is one of the world's safest cities to wander around; no wonder it's so easy to feel at home here.

The White City ★★★

Tel Aviv is home to the world's largest collection of buildings constructed in the **Bauhaus** style, a UNESCO-protected area known as the **White City**. The area is bordered by Allenby Street in the south, Begin Road in the east, the Yarkon River to the north and the Mediterranean to the west, although in reality, most of the finest examples are along **Rothschild Boulevard**.

More than 4000 properties were built in the Bauhaus style. The city's layout was actually planned by a Scotsman, **Sir Patrick Geddes** (*see* panel, this page), but

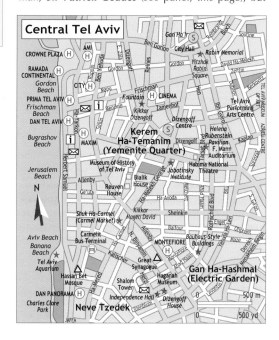

Left: *Street plaque marking the boundary of the White City, the world's richest concentration of Bauhaus architecture.*

individual buildings were designed by Jewish architects who had studied in Europe before returning to Palestine in the 1920s to live in the growing Tel Aviv, and then, in the 1930s, those fleeing the rise of Nazi Germany.

Between 1500 and 2000 buildings in Tel Aviv have been protected as examples of the world's greatest concentration of Bauhaus structures. Some of the buildings are obvious, with their gleaming, restored façades and clean, minimalist lines. Others have not been touched in a century and are crumbling, with scruffy gardens and broken panes of glass.

The architectural style of Bauhaus and its close relatives is characterized by asymmetry, simplicity and functionality, with solid balconies, flat roofs and, in the stairwells, narrow windows that curiously resemble the glass on a thermometer, stacked on top of one another. On first sight, the buildings appear stark, but if you look closely, many have exquisite details – graceful pillars, the use of glass bricks to allow light in, simple motifs reflecting the architect's individual passions, although the style does not permit any unnecessary adornment. Needless to say, these buildings are highly coveted as residential property and command huge prices with their high ceilings, flat roofs (where many people have planted gardens or built extensions) and big windows.

BAUHAUS

Stattliches Bauhaus was a school in Germany that combined crafts and the fine arts, and was famous for the approach to design and architecture that it embodied. It operated from 1919 to 1933 and was founded by **Walter Gropius** in the city of Weimar.

The stark, minimalist Bauhaus style went on to become one of the strongest influences on modernist architecture and contemporary design. Schools existed in Weimar, Dessau and Berlin but the movement was closed by the Nazi regime and its followers took their style abroad to cities like Tel Aviv.

The city itself was originally designed as a clever grid system, with many blocks of buildings as individual islands. Each block was surrounded by one-way streets – even though Geddes's design was conceived when the motor car was in its infancy, he had a prophetic view on its success and his design was aimed at reducing traffic congestion. Each block had a green space and each house is detached, the better to withstand the summer heat. Many are angled towards the Mediterranean, to catch the sea breezes.

Each house can only occupy 50% of its plot, so houses tend to be built on pillars with gardens underneath. The smarter ones, once inhabited by European immigrants, have fish ponds and fountains. Many, however, are in a state of disrepair following years of protected tenancy agreements and neglectful landlords. Look closely at the wood, bevelled glass and tiles in the old houses – much of it was imported from Germany, when immigrants fleeing the Nazis had to divest themselves of their assets before leaving. They couldn't export cash, but they could – and did – bring building materials to Israel.

Below: *Dizengoff Circle, a popular meeting place, has an unusual rotating fountain in the centre.*

Dizengoff Circle Area ★★

Once the fashion and food highlight of Tel Aviv, this still-glamorous boulevard is the place to sit in a pavement café and people-watch or to browse through the many chic designer shops. Eat your way through delicious Viennese pastries, fruit-juice cocktails, Hungarian blinis, pastrami and falafel. If you're intrigued by the Bauhaus movement, call in at the **Bauhaus Center** at 99

Dizengoff Street for information about the movement as well as paintings, furniture for sale, miniatures, photography and other tasteful Tel Aviv souvenirs.

The focal point of all this is Dizengoff Circle, a raised piazza with an unusual **fountain** at its centre. The fountain is a series of coloured, cog-like rings which rotate. Every hour, on the hour, there's a musical display with jets of water and a flame. A few streets to the south is the Dizengoff Centre, a busy shopping centre complete with restaurants and cinemas.

Walking Tour: Rothschild Boulevard Area ★★★

Much of Rothschild Boulevard, one of the main avenues bisecting the city, is a UNESCO World Heritage Site, thanks to its beautiful Modernist architecture. The street itself, which cuts through the financial district, is a broad sweep divided down the middle by a pedestrian area, lined with shady trees and what used to be little newspaper kiosks. Today, they're trendy sushi bars and tiny coffee shops.

Start at the bottom of the street. There are a few sights to see before the real density of Bauhaus buildings begins. No. 8 Rothschild is opposite the **Founders' Monument**, commemorating the establishment of the city's first well. No. 16 is **Independence Hall**, former residence of Meir Dizengoff, in which the independent State of Israel was declared by the then prime minister, David Ben-Gurion. It's open to the public 09:00–14:00 Sunday–Thursday.

The peculiar mix of styles of No. 46 – ornate balconies and a minaret – attracted the attention of the **Soviet Ambassador**, who chose to base the embassy there until diplomatic relations were severed in 1953.

The **Haganah Museum** at No. 23 provides a fascinating glimpse into the methods used by the Israeli Defence Force in manufacturing arms and concealing them from the British when Palestine was under British Mandate. Open 08:00–16:00 Sunday–Thursday. No. 89 and No. 91, meanwhile, are typical examples of the German Bauhaus school of architecture.

THE GREAT ISRAELI BREAKFAST

Breakfasts in Israel never cease to amaze visitors. As most hotels are kosher, meat and dairy are not mixed, and breakfast is a dairy extravaganza. As well as fruits and cereals, you'll see seven or eight types of cheese on a typical buffet; yoghurt; cream cheese; stuffed vine leaves; salads; platters of smoked salmon; freshly baked pittas with olive oil and garlic; and tempting, sticky pastries, from filled croissants to elaborate cakes. Fill up at breakfast and you can save money by getting by on just a falafel for lunch.

ECLECTIC STYLE

During the 1920s the fashionable building style was eclectic. European immigrants with money and the dream of a new Utopia were streaming into what was then Palestine, bringing with them their own architectural ideas. The results were a complete mixture of styles: domes, arches, big windows to catch the breeze and expressions of love for Judaism – menorahs, Stars of David and biblical images. You can see these buildings around the old commercial centre of the city.

Above: *One of the modernist mansions on the elegant Rothschild Boulevard.*

Now the real concentration of the White City begins. Start just beyond the junction of Rothschild and Allenby and work your way north. On Rothschild, numbers 67, 71, 82 and 84 are all superb examples of the Bauhaus style: the cubist look and pinkish *waschputz* (washed plaster) of **Samuelson House** at No. 67; the nod to the great architect, **Le Corbusier**, in the façade of **Krieger House** at No. 71; the smooth lines of **Rubinsky House** at No. 82 (which has been painted out of context with the style but still looks wonderful); and more Le Corbusier influences at the wave-like **Engel House** at No. 84. This was the first house to be planned on stilts and today it has a roof garden, originally intended as a communal space for the residents.

There are more examples in the residential streets around Rothschild. Check out the **Sharbal House** at 78 Ahad Haam, with its angular, railed balconies, and the **Elyashav House** on Maze, a symmetrical house with glazed bricks creating horizontal accents.

The **Yerachmilevsky House** at No. 24 Balfour is built on stilts and has a pergola on the roof. Inside, the courtyard and stairwells are surprisingly ornate for the period, with an Art Deco fish pond and decorative ceramic tiles.

Walk up to Melchett Street and check out the **Landa House**, which has angular and curved balconies, liberal use of glass tiles to allow light in, and a rooftop pergola. Cross over Rothschild to Engel Street and look at numbers 5 and 8. The **Aginsky House**, No. 5, has glass-brick windows, allowing its stairwell to flood with light, and a cleverly extended eastern side to catch the sea breezes. The nearby **Hendel House**, with its rounded balconies, is inspired by a ship.

Next, you can take a detour up Sheinkin Street to see the **Rubinsky House**, No. 65, a fine example of the use of *kratzputz*, or scraped plaster, which glitters in the sunshine.

Back on Rothschild, after the intersection with Sheinkin Street, there are four notable protected buildings at numbers 115, 117, 118 and 119. The Russian architect who designed the **Goldenberg House** at No. 115 was an expert in *waschputz*, the technique of covering the façade with tiny stones and coating them with washed plaster to create a pebbledash effect. Note the extension on top of the house; a lot of the protected buildings have been extended upwards, but the extensions are always recessed to protect the original lines of the building.

Nahalat Binyamin ★★

Every Tuesday and Friday, there's an **arts and crafts market** in a couple of pedestrianized streets near the big Carmel Market. This is a great place to browse the stalls for handmade jewellery, Judaica with a contemporary twist (amusing clocks, fridge magnets and so on), wood-carved items, scented candles and soaps, plants, pots and paintings, including a couple of places selling beautiful black-and-white photographic prints of Israel. Get there early as it gets very busy. The street is lined with cafés for breakfast (the market is open 10:00–17:00, Tuesday and Friday).

Carmel Market ★★★

Nearby is the city's most famous market, **Ha-Carmel**, best known for its fruit and vegetables but actually selling everything from pots and pans to clothing and

---

SHABBAT IN TEL AVIV

The Jewish Sabbath extends from sunset on Friday until the time when three stars have appeared in the sky on Saturday evening. In religious Jerusalem this means everything winds down from mid-afternoon on Fridays, and Saturdays are very quiet, with most shops and attractions closed. In Tel Aviv, which is far more secular, late afternoon on Fridays will be quiet but the bars and clubs will be busy later on. Saturday is a day for breakfasting with friends on Sheinkin Street, doing the weekly food shop in Carmel Market and later heading for the beach. Some museums may be closed, but generally visitors won't be affected.

Above: *Pomegranate and orange juice bars are dotted all over the colourful Carmel Market.*

household cleaning equipment. The fresh fruit and vegetable section is an eye-opener: pomegranates the size of footballs, great big mounds of enormous scarlet strawberries and mountains of oranges from Jaffa. There are cheese stalls, pastry stalls piled high with oozing baklava, chocolate shops, falafel stalls and, in another (thankfully more distant) section, meat stalls. Don't miss the chance to try a freshly squeezed orange and pomegranate juice – every other stall in the fruit section is a juice bar. Also look out for stalls selling *borekas*, a savoury puff pastry triangle filled with spinach, cheese or potato. Originally Turkish, they're an old favourite of the Sephardi Jews – and now Israelis.

Sheinkin Street ★★

Sheinkin has long since taken over from Dizengoff as the coolest fashion street in the city, lined on both sides with designer shops; not *haute couture*, but young, fashionable Israeli labels like **Ronen Chen**, whose fluid dresses and separates are perfect for the working woman, and **Daniela Lehavi**, a shop packed with the softest leather bags and shoes. **Michal Negrin** sells vintage-inspired jewellery and accessories, as well as pretty items for the home, while **Sabon** is the place to call for scented candles and soaps. There are sports shops, grungy teenage fashions, tattoo parlours and bookshops, too – in effect, everything.

Sheinkin is right next to a very picturesque, tree-lined, up-and-coming residential neighbourhood, the inhabitants of which emerge on Saturday mornings for breakfast and coffee in the many street cafés. For a bit of living history, **Café Tamar** (*see* panel, page 51) has been on the corner of Sheinkin and Ahad Haam streets since the 1940s, a popular gathering place for left-wing thinkers, artists and writers. There are faded political posters all over the walls and the original formica table cloths on every table. It's still a place where you might spot famous politicians and political activists.

Gan Ha-Hashmal ★

Tel Aviv is a cutting-edge centre for talented young designers and you can find their ateliers dotted around the city. You have to know where they are, though, as many are tucked away in small, unassuming neigh-bourhoods, unable to afford the high rents in trendy places like Neve Tzedek.

Gan Ha-Hashmal, or the **Electric Garden**, to the east of the southern end of Rothschild, is such an area, recently gentrified, with a scruffy little park at its centre. In the streets around here are such treasures as **Kisim**, whose gorgeous leather bags were featured in the 2008 movie *Sex and the City*, and on Levontin Street, **Ruby Star** for more bags, belts and jewellery. **Mira Mory** is another jewellery workshop, producing delicate gold and silver pieces, while **Sevilia** is a designer jewellery store specializing in the unusual combination of gold and leather. You do have to pound the streets to find what you want as some of the workshops are very small – but they are all welcoming, you can see the designers at work and the prices are unbeatable, given the standard of the goods.

Yemenite Quarter or Kerem Ha-Temanim ★★

If you're visiting Carmel Market, take a stroll westwards towards the sea through the **Yemenite Vineyard**, a quaint old neigh-bourhood bounded by Ge'ula Street, Carmel Market and Allenby Street. There's no evidence of a vineyard here any more, but the early Yemenite settlers, who moved here in 1903, planted vines and built

Below: *Café Tamar is a Tel Aviv institution, its décor unchanged since the 1950s.*

YEMENITE CUISINE

Yemenite cuisine is a variation on the Middle Eastern theme with a number of delicious, unique characteristics. You'll find the usual fare of hummus and spicy dips to start with, followed by meat dishes – meatballs in spicy tomato sauce is typical. *Jachnun*, a kind of deep-fried dough served with a boiled egg and spicy tomato sauce, is a favourite Saturday morning dish, while *malawah* or *lechuch* is a bread baked in a clay kiln, served with lentil soup (*shorbat ada*). Mixed grill of liver and kidney is also popular. Most main courses of beef, chicken, fish or vegetables incorporate *hawa'age*, a spicy mixture that consists of turmeric, cumin, coriander and black pepper. Expect garnishes of fresh garlic, onion, tomatoes and coriander and some relishes which pack a punch of their own: *hilbeh*, a spicy dip made from freshly ground fenugreek, and *schug*, a combination of fresh coriander and chilli.

simple houses out of mud and mortar, staking their claim in what would become the new Tel Aviv. Like other previously run-down areas, though, the **Kerem**, as it's known, is becoming a desirable place to live. Old houses are being renovated and prices are going up.

A walk here is still, however, like stepping back in time, through narrow alleys where life goes on in the streets. Save your appetite for fresh, home-made falafel and vegetable soup, warm pitta, meatballs and stuffed potatoes, all from tiny, hole-in-the-wall establishments.

Lilienblum Street ★

Lilienblum Street extends from the edge of hip Neve Tzedek to Allenby Street through the financial district, such as that is – Tel Aviv doesn't really have a single concentration of financial institutions like London and New York. Lilienblum is the place to head for bar-crawling at night – not in a drunken, sleazy way but from one über-cool establishment to the next. Thursday nights here are packed. Try **Mish Mish**, dark, loud and hip, with seating in plush leather booths and a resident DJ, or **Abraxas**, always packed, with loud music from resident DJs. The ultimate experience is **Nanutchka**, with its pink neon signs, padded red ceiling and rabbit warren of tiny rooms, packed solid with people shouting over the sound of loud Gregorian pop music.

Right: *Any time of day is a good time to walk and play on Tel Aviv's long, sandy beaches.*

Beaches of Central Tel Aviv ★★
Frischman Beach
Right in front of the colourful **Dan Hotel** (a very useful landmark if you're running or walking along the sand and aren't familiar with the city), this is a luxury beach with good bars and cafés nearby and with great views of Jaffa to the south and the northern beaches in the opposite direction.

Jerusalem Beach
This is one of the widest beaches, with sun umbrellas to rent as well as plenty of cafés and restaurants along the neighbouring Herbert Samuel Street. The amount of space means this is the place to turn up for an impromptu soccer or volleyball game; there's usually one going on.

Banana Beach
There's a café here of the same name, turning into a popular chillout bar at sunset and showing movies on a giant screen on summer nights. Banana Beach ends at the derelict Dolphinarium (*see* page 39).

Above: *Jerusalem Beach is one of the most popular and a likely spot for an impromptu game of beach volleyball.*

Central Tel Aviv at a Glance

BEST TIMES TO VISIT

Tel Aviv is a year-round destination but if you want to sit on the beach, March to October is best. Avoid July and August as it can get very humid. September is the period of a lot of the main Jewish holidays, so museums and attractions may be closed at odd hours.

GETTING THERE

Ben Gurion International, Israel's main airport, is situated 20km (12.5 miles) from the city, served by buses, trains and taxis. There's a small domestic airport, **Sde Dov**, north of the city, with flights to other parts of Israel. **Buses** in Tel Aviv are run by Dan, tel: 03 639 4444, www.dan.co.il and Egged, tel: 03 694 8888, www.egged.co.il Israel Railways operates frequent **trains** from the airport to three stops in Tel Aviv, tel: 03 611 7000, www.rail.co.il **Taxis** wait at the airport and operate on a meter.

GETTING AROUND

Tel Aviv has an efficient **bus** service, run by Dan (see above) and also with some Egged buses (see above). **Taxis** are inexpensive and can be hailed on the street. **Walking** is pleasant outside the main summer season; you can walk all the way from north Tel Aviv to Jaffa on the beach. It's not worth hiring a **car** unless you plan to leave

the city and need transport for day trips. **Car Rental:** Avis, 13 Ha-Yarkon St, tel: 1 700 700 222; Budget, 99 Ha-Yarkon St, tel: 1 700 704 141. Be green and hire a **bicycle** instead, tel: 03 544 2292, www.rentabikeisrael.com

WHERE TO STAY

LUXURY
Hilton Tel Aviv, Independence Park, tel: 03 520 2222, www1.hilton.com Long-established five-star business hotel, which also attracts leisure guests thanks to its great location on the beach.
Dan Tel Aviv, 99 Ha-Yarkon St, tel: 03 520 2525, www.danhotels.com The Dan is probably Tel Aviv's most famous hotel, with a rooftop swimming pool and contemporary rooms. It serves a legendary breakfast buffet.

MID-RANGE
Prima Tel Aviv, 105 Ha-Yarkon St, tel: 03 520 6666, www.prima-hotels-israel.com Moderately priced hotel in enviable beachfront location, with its own kosher Thai restaurant.
Hotel Cinema, 1 Zamenhof Street, tel: 03 520 7100, fax: 03 520 7101, www.cinemahotel.com This fantastic, characterful hotel is located at Dizengoff Circle, housed in a former

cinema. Old cinema posters and memorabilia are everywhere and the building retains its original Art Deco features.
Hotel Montefiore, 36 Montefiore St, tel: 03 564 6100, www.hotelmontefiore.co.il The Montefiore is a beautiful boutique bolthole, housed in a 1920s mansion, with 12 suites and an ultra-trendy bar and restaurant.

BUDGET
Maxim Hotel, 86 Ha-Yarkon St, Tel Aviv, tel: 03 517 3721, fax: 03 517 3726, www.maxim-htl-ta.co.il This reasonably priced small hotel is situated in the heart of the action, near the nightlife and shopping, right on the beach.
City Hotel, 9 Mapu Street (just off Ben Yehuda Street), tel: 03 524 6253, www.atlas.co.il Small hotel in a quiet street just off the main promenade.

WHERE TO EAT

Pasha, 8 Ha-Arba'a St, tel: 03 561 7778. Kosher food is served in this lavish Turkish restaurant in an amazingly ornate setting.
Max Brenner, 45 Rothschild Blvd, tel: 03 560 4570. This is the best place to go if you are looking for chocolate. There are chocolate cocktails, fondues, puddings, chocolate coffees and all manner of chocolate bars, made on the premises.

Central Tel Aviv at a Glance

Sushisamba TLV, 27 Ha-Barzel St, Ramat Ha-Chayal, tel: 03 644 4345, http://sushisamba. rest-e.co.il Japanese meets Brazilian and Peruvian cuisine in this ultra-hip outpost of the well-known US restaurant.

Orna and Ella, 33 Sheinkin St, tel: 03 525 2085. This is a Tel Aviv classic café; very romantic and very fashionable, Orna and Ella offers French and Medi-terranean dishes.

Buddha Burger, 86 Ibn Gavirol St, tel: 03 522 3040; also at 21 Yehuda Ha-Levi Street, tel: 03 510 1222, www.buddhaburgers.co.il Brilliantly creative veggie food is served at this eatery, from salads and burritos to stir fries and 'burgers'.

Café Tamar, 57 Sheinkin Street near Ahad Haam, tel: 03 685 2376. Famous hang-out of politicians, writers and activists. Straight out of the 1950s. Basic café fare and great atmosphere.

Medina, 18 Mallan St, no tel. Basic but interesting restaurant for lunch in the Yemenite Quarter. Try the meat soup, schnitzel or hummus and sample the hilbe curry-flavoured paste. Unusual!

SHOPPING

Sheinkin Street is one of the city's busiest shopping areas, featuring Israeli designers, boutique interiors shops and a large number of establish-ments selling accessories. If it's cutting-edge design you're

after, the best thing to do is to wander around the **Gan Ha-Hashmal** (Electric Garden) area (Levontin and Ha-Hashmal streets) where there are lots of up-and-coming clothing and jewellery designers and also some amazing leather shops. Bigger and more mainstream shops are located around **Dizengoff Centre**. For fruit, vegetables, souvenirs and general household goods, you can't beat the vibrant **Carmel Market**. For gifts to take home, art, fun Judaica and pretty household items, **Nahalat Binyamin** market on Friday mornings is the best place to go.

TOURS AND EXCURSIONS

There are free walking tours of the White City every Saturday at 11:00. Groups meet at 46 Rothschild Boulevard (on the corner of Shadal Street). This tour focuses on the modern architectural styles of the 1930s in one of the 'White City' main areas, along Rothschild Boulevard. There is no need to book in advance. On Fridays at 10:00 there are also tours leaving from the Tel Aviv Bauhaus Center, 99

Dizengoff St, tel: 03 522 0249, www.bauhaus-center.com Alternatively, you can hire a **specialist guide**. Paule Rakower is a White City expert and local resident; tel: 03 546 4917, e-mail: krpaule@hotmail.com

The Association for Tourism Tel Aviv-Jaffa, tel: 03 516 6188, www.visit-tlv.com Open Sun–Thu 09:30–17:30.

USEFUL CONTACTS

Ben Gurion International Airport, flight information, tel: 03 972 3344.
Tourist Information Offices:
Ben Gurion Airport, tel: 03 975 4260;
46 Herbert Samuel St, tel: 03 516 6188.
Tel Aviv-Jaffa Municipality, Yitzhak Rabin Square, tel: 03 521 8438. Also look out for the new mobile tourist information booth – a Segway, which tours the popular sites dispensing help and information.

Local information: visit www.visit-tlv.com
Police, tel: 100.
Magen David Adom First Aid, tel: 101.
Fire Department, tel: 102.

TEL AVIV	J	F	M	A	M	J	J	A	S	O	N	D
AVERAGE TEMP °C	18	19	20	22	25	28	30	30	31	29	24	19
AVERAGE TEMP °F	65	66	68	72	77	83	86	86	89	84	76	66
RAINFALL mm	80	80	56	15	0	0	0	0	0	16	48	62
RAINFALL in	3.1	3.1	2.2	0.6	0	0	0	0	0	0.63	1.9	2.3
DAYS OF RAINFALL	11	11	8	4	0	0	0	0	0	5	10	11

4
North Tel Aviv

While most of the famous neighbourhoods are in the southern sector of the city, the north is home to some of the finest museums, as well as ultra-modern architecture, from the shimmering **Azrieli Towers**, once the tallest buildings in the Middle East, to the revitalized **port** area with its cool outdoor lounges and undulating wooden decking.

The art and music scenes come alive in this northern sector of the city. The magnificent **Tel Aviv Museum of Art** and the futuristic **Performing Arts Centre** alongside it are testament to the rich cultural life here.

There are many lessons to be learned about Israel's history, too, from the poignant memorial to Yitzhak Rabin in **Yitzhak Rabin Square** to the fascinating **Eretz Israel Museum**, telling the story of life in the Land of Israel, and the **Museum of the Jewish Diaspora**, a subject close to the heart of any Jew visiting Israel.

The northern areas have their frivolous side, too, in the huge, green expanse of **Ha-Yarkon Park**, one of the finest city parks in the world, where locals escape to listen to the birds, paddle boats on the lake, have picnics under the trees and listen to the free concerts on summer nights. The redeveloped **Tel Aviv Port** has brought new life to the nights here, creating prestigious bars, clubs and restaurants to rival any around the Mediterranean's glamorous hot spots. And then there are the **beaches** – mile upon mile of golden sand, a magnet to swimmers, surfers, dog-walkers, families, lovers and friends.

DON'T MISS

★★★ **New Port:** nights at the revived port, packed with clubs and bars.
★★★ **Tel Aviv Museum of Art:** an excellent museum, housed in three buildings.
★★★ **The Performing Arts Centre:** go there, even if you only visit the lobby.
★★ Pay a visit to **Yitzhak Rabin Square**.
★★ Go for a picnic in **Ha-Yarkon Park**.

Opposite: *The colourful Dan Hotel is a Tel Aviv landmark.*

Yitzhak Rabin Square ★★

Yitzhak Rabin Square, overlooked by the concrete block of the **City Hall**, has been named after the much-loved Israeli prime minister, an important architect of the Middle East peace process and winner of the Nobel Peace Prize. Rabin was killed on 4 November 1995 by three bullets fired by right-wing Israeli radical Yigal Amir, who was opposed to Rabin's signing of the Oslo Accords. The assassination took place at a packed rally in the square in support of the government's peace policy.

The bleak-looking monument to Rabin was erected a year after his murder. Created by the sculptor **Yael Ben-Artzi**, the memorial is made of 16 basalt stones from the **Golan Heights**. The stones are embedded in the earth to symbolize Rabin's roots and his deep connection to the land (he was Israel's first native-born prime minister). The stones are set at varying heights and lit from below by a red light, suggesting an eternal flame. Graffiti, most of it in Hebrew, surrounds the memorial. Thousands gather here every year on the anniversary of Rabin's death – a sobering moment. The square is also, however, a symbol of Israel's desire for peace. In 2009, as part of the city's centenary celebrations, it was completely covered by a carpet of flowers.

Right: *Assassinated prime minister Yitzhak Rabin's memory lives on.*

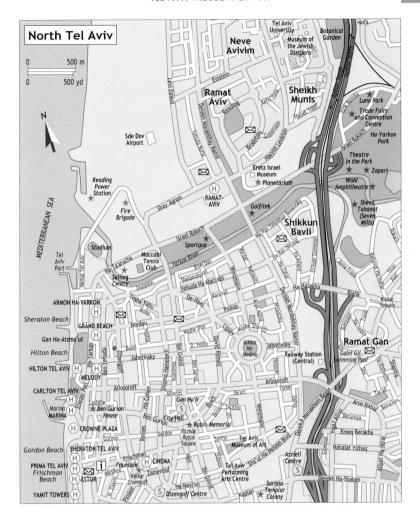

Tel Aviv Museum of Art ★★★

The wonderful Tel Aviv Museum of Art is housed in three buildings. The **Helena Rubenstein Pavilion** at the top of Rothschild Boulevard houses temporary exhibitions of contemporary art. Nearby there's the **Art Education Centre** and on Sha'ul Ha-Melekh Boulevard

Above: *Contemporary art lovers should spend a day at the Tel Aviv Museum of Art.*
Opposite: *The ultra-modern Opera House is an attraction in itself.*

is the museum's **main site**, with permanent collections of Israeli and modern art and a large European section from the 16th to the 19th centuries. This really is an excellent museum, intelligently laid out, modern, spacious and extremely family-friendly; on a Friday, you will see a lot of families here, with special workshops and drawing areas for children.

For lovers of contemporary art, this place is a paradise and a breathtaking example of Israel's deep connections with serious collectors all over the world, many of whom have loaned pieces to the museum. There is work by Paul Cezanne, Alfred Sisley, Henri Edmond Cross, Pierre Bonnard, Henri Matisse, Amedeo Modigliani and Marc Chagall in the **Simon and Marie Jaglom Collection**, which focuses on French art of the turn of the century, while the **Moshe and Sara Mayer Collection** features pieces by Degas, Renoir, Monet, Pissarro, Van Gogh, Gauguin, Cezanne, Miró and big names from various other genres including Cubism and German Expressionism. You'll find far more, though; allow at least half a day. Open 10:00–16:00 Monday, Wednesday, Saturday; 10:00–22:00 Tuesday, Thursday; 10:00–14:00 Friday; closed Sunday.

The Tel Aviv Performing Arts Centre ★★★

Next to the main museum building (you can walk between the two) is the graceful **Tel Aviv Performing Arts Centre (TAPAC)**, residence of the **Israeli Opera**. Designed by the late **Ya'akov Rechter**, the building was opened to the public in October 1994 and is the focal point for cultural and artistic events in Tel Aviv. Take a look into the foyer, a futuristic, curvy space created by architect-designer **Ron Arad**. Everything is curved, from the stairs to the box office, the chairs, the wall of glass and the bar of the chic little café. There are temporary art exhibitions in the foyer, various performances at the small amphitheatre and an impressive music shop.

On Fridays at 11:00 there are free backstage tours (meet in the foyer) and, more excitingly, you can book onto a special tour during performances that takes you backstage one hour before the curtain rises to see the last-minute preparations. It may not be in English but opera doesn't really need translation. Reserve in advance on tel: 03 692 7777.

The foyer is open Sunday–Thursday 09:30–20:30 and Fridays 09:30–13:00, as well as during performances (www.israel-opera.co.il).

MINISTER MEIR

Golda Meir (1898–1978) was one of the founders of the State of Israel. While in her teens she became a Zionist, and in 1921 she and her husband immigrated to Palestine. She was a signatory to the **Proclamation of the Independence of the State of Israel** in 1948 and served as her country's first minister to the USSR, as well as minister of labour and social insurance for Israel. In 1956 she became minister of foreign affairs. She served, successively, as secretary-general of the Mapai Party and of the United Israel Labour Party from 1966–68. She was prime minister from 1969 to 1974, when she resigned amid controversy over Israel's lack of preparedness in the Yom Kippur War of 1973.

Eretz Israel Museum ★★

North of the Yarkon River in extensive grounds is the Eretz Israel Museum, which tells the story of the Land of Israel through an array of exhibits of archaeology, ethnography, folklore, Judaica, cultural history and local identity, traditional crafts and practical arts. It's built around **Tel Qasile**, an ancient mound rich in archaeological treasures, many of which are on display in the museum complex. The permanent displays include a beautiful Mosaic Hall, an Iron-Age oil press, a working crafts area and a working

THE JEWISH DIASPORA

The Jewish Diaspora, or scattering, began in 587BC, when the kingdom of Judea was conquered by the Babylonians, who destroyed the Temple in Jerusalem and exiled the Jews. When it was rebuilt and the Jews allowed to return, many remained in Babylon. The destruction of the Second Temple by the Romans in AD70 and the second expulsion caused the Jewish population to spread throughout the Roman Empire. In the Middle Ages, fleeing persecution, many settled in Eastern Europe, and in the 20th century, in the Americas. To this day, Jews have remained scattered worldwide; of the 13.2 million in the world, only five and a half million live in Israel, although all have the right to return. About six million Jews live in North America and 1.5 million in Europe. France has the third-largest Jewish population in the world and there are size-able communities in South Africa and Australia.

flour mill. There's also a planetarium. The museum provides a fascinating insight into history and is also a good family day out. Open Sunday–Wednesday 10:00–16:00, Friday–Saturday 10:00–14:00.

Tel Aviv University ★

Lovers of modern architecture should pay a visit to the huge university campus in the northern suburb of **Ramat Aviv**, where there are free guided tours of the complex, which includes fine examples of Bauhaus, 1970s, post- and neo-modernist structures. The campus is also dotted with 50 impressive sculptures. Tours depart Mondays at 11:00 from the Dionon Bookstore at Entin Square (Levanon and Einstein streets); no appoint-ment is needed.

Museum of the Jewish Diaspora ★

While you're on the campus, visit **Beth Hatefutsoth**, the **Nahum Goldmann Museum of the Jewish Diaspora**, which tells the story of the Jewish people living in scores of different countries for centuries and millennia, right up to the present. The continuity of the Jewish people is told through photographs, audiovisual and written dis-plays, tracing their scattering all over the world and providing a valuable research tool for many people try-ing to trace their family trees. There are guided tours in English (book in advance through www.bh.org.il). Open Sunday–Thursday 10:00–19:00; Friday 09:00–14:00.

The New Port ★★

Tel Aviv Port, once a run-down area just to the south of the mouth of the Yarkon River, has been transformed beyond recognition in recent years. Now, it's a super-chic shopping, dining and clubbing area, the old warehouses transformed into lounge bars and big retail outlets, all set along miles of warm, wooden board-walk, curiously undulating in places, making it a mecca for skateboarders. By day, it's all shopping and lunch by the water, while at night the area is transformed into a cool hangout for the young and the beautiful, with

Left: *Tel Aviv has been carefully designed with plenty of parks and green spaces such as this one in the suburb of Ramat Gan.*

outdoor lounge bars playing chill-out music and, later, fancy clubs like Whisky Go Go.

A bridge across the Yarkon River connects the port to the old **Reading Power Station**, whose cavernous interior now serves as an exciting venue for post-modern design and art exhibitions.

Near the bridge is a foot and bicycle path, the **Yarkon Promenade**, that heads east along the banks of the river into the Ha-Yarkon Park, Tel Aviv's green lung, with lakes, woods and playing fields.

Ha-Yarkon Park ★★

Ha-Yarkon Park, which runs along the banks of the Yarkon River where it divides the north of the city from the rest, and down the whole eastern side of the city centre, is where locals go to play as a change from the beach – 400ha (nearly 1000 acres) of gardens, ponds, trees and a huge playground. You'll find bike rental, mini-golf, pony rides, train rides for children, a puppet theatre, ornamental lakes and the **Memadion Water Park** for cooling off on a hot day. Teens gather here to play soccer, basketball, baseball and to skateboard, and there's an impressive climbing wall. In summer,

THE NEW PORT

Tel Aviv Port was founded in 1936 but over the decades fell into decline. The recent transformation has turned the port area into a focus of culture, entertainment and leisure activities, with numerous restaurants, big warehouse-style shops and even a women-only spa. The huge wooden deck surrounding the port area covers 14,000m^2 (150,695 sq ft) and is the largest of its kind in Israel, designed in a unique wave-like shape inspired by the sand dunes of the early days of Tel Aviv, 100 years ago.

concerts, many of them free, are held in the park – **Sir Paul McCartney** performed here, as did **Milan's La Scala**.

Sarona Templar Colony ★

Sarona Garden on Kaplan Street, in front of the Azrieli Centre, is a former German agricultural village, established by the **Templars** in 1871. The simple stone houses were crumbling until recently, but a restoration is going on to turn the area into a real 'village', with outdoor cafés and gardens around the original single-storey houses. It doesn't look like much at the moment but is considered of high enough historical value for some of the houses to have been physically moved, brick by brick, to accommodate the new dual carriageway leading out of the city towards Jerusalem.

Above: *The Azrieli Towers are some of the tallest buildings in the Middle East.*

Azrieli Centre ★

Built in the shapes of a circle, a square and a triangle, the three shimmering glass Azrieli Towers are among the tallest buildings in the Middle East, although the Moshe Aviv Tower in nearby Ramat Gan takes the record for Israel's tallest building. They're nonetheless pleasing to look at, as far as skyscrapers go, housing a mix of residential, commercial and hotel development.

There's a huge shopping mall here (although you could be anywhere in the world); the main reason to visit is to ride the lift up to the **observation platform** on the 49th floor (open shopping hours Sunday–Friday). On a clear day you can see all along the coast and as far east as the **Judean Hills**.

Beaches of North Tel Aviv ★★★

Heading south from the New Port you'll find a long string of beautiful, clean, sandy beaches. Each has its own character – and attracts its own crowd.

Sheraton Beach, or Mezzizzim Beach

The most northerly of the beaches, this is clean and has facilities and a children's play area, although the water is cloudy as the Yarkon River drains into the sea here. The beach is noisy, too, with aircraft overhead from the small, regional Sde Dov Airport.

Religious Beach

This small area south of Sheraton Beach is for the **ultra-Orthodox**, with separate bathing days for men and women (Sunday, Tuesday and Thursday for women, Monday, Wednesday and Friday for men). Saturday is a mixed day, when the strictly religious would not in any case go to the beach. The reality is that this beach is popular with women who want to **sunbathe topless** but don't want to attract unwanted male attention.

Atzmout Beach and Hilton Beach

So called because of its proximity to the Hilton Hotel, this beach is one where dogs are allowed to run free. It has a cheery atmosphere as the dogs' owners socialize, and surfers love the big waves. This area is also an unofficial gay beach and, as such, lures a glamorous crowd. You'll see a lot of people playing *matkot* here, the unofficial national sport of Israel, essentially a version of beach paddleball, played in the shallow water.

Gordon Beach

Located close to the city centre, this is a wide stretch of clean sand with some good cafés, a Ben & Jerry's ice cream stall and plenty of sunloungers to rent. The **Lalaland Café** is a popular sunset spot, with cocktails and uninterrupted views. Gordon Beach merges into **Frischman Beach** in front of the Dan Hotel, and this is one of the busiest and most popular spots along this coast.

North Tel Aviv at a Glance

BEST TIMES TO VISIT

Tel Aviv is a city which can be visited year-round but if you want to sit on the beach, March to October is the best time. Avoid July and August as it can get very humid. September is the period during which a lot of the main Jewish holidays occur, so museums and attractions may be closed at odd hours.

GETTING THERE

Ben Gurion International, Israel's main airport, is situated 20km (12.5 miles) from the city, served by buses, trains and taxis. There's a small domestic airport, **Sde Dov**, north of the city, with flights to other parts of Israel. **Buses** in Tel Aviv are run by Dan, tel: 03 639 4444, www.dan.co.il and Egged, tel: 03 694 8888, www.egged.co.il Israel Railways operates frequent **trains** from the airport to three stops in Tel Aviv, tel: 03 611 7000, www.rail.co.il **Taxis** wait at the airport and operate on a meter.

GETTING AROUND

Tel Aviv has an efficient **bus** service, run by Dan (*see above*) and also with some Egged buses (*see above*). **Taxis** are inexpensive and can be hailed on the street. **Walking** is pleasant outside the main summer season; you can walk all the way from north Tel Aviv to Jaffa on the beach. It's not worth hiring a **car** unless you plan to leave the city and need transport for day trips.
Car Rental: Avis, 13 Ha-Yarkon St, tel: 1 700 700 222; Budget, 99 Ha-Yarkon St, tel: 1 700 704 141. Be green and hire a **bicycle** instead, tel: 03 544 2292, www.rentabikeisrael.com There are some wonderful cycle trails through Ha-Yarkon Park which are safe for both adults and children.

WHERE TO STAY

LUXURY
Hilton Tel Aviv, Independence Park, tel: 03 520 2222, www1.hilton.com The Hilton is a Tel Aviv institution, located right by the sea in Independence Park. It is a big business hotel with good leisure facilities, too. The breakfasts here are justifiably famous.
Crowne Plaza, 145 Ha-Yarkon Street, tel: 03 520 1111, www.ichotelsgroup.com Luxury, 246-room hotel right on the beach. It has two restaurants, including one Asian.
Carlton Tel Aviv, 10 Eliezer Peri Street, tel: 03 520 1818, www.carlton.co.il Large five-star business/leisure hotel with a beach restaurant and a swimming pool.

MID-RANGE
Grand Beach, 250 Ha-Yarkon St, tel: 03 543 3333. Business/leisure hotel with outdoor pool, overlooking both Independence Park and the sea.
Marina Hotel,167 Ha-Yarkon Street, tel: 03 521 1777, www.marina-telaviv.co.il This business/leisure hotel overlooks the marina. It has an outdoor pool and a restaurant.
Melody Hotel, 220 Ha-Yarkon Street, tel: 03 521 5300, www.atlas.co.il This funky, arty boutique hotel with a gorgeous roof terrace overlooking the sea is a great alternative to one of the bigger hotels.

BUDGET
Armon Ha-Yarkon, 268 Ha-Yarkon Street, tel: 03 605 5271, www.armon-hotel.com Small, 24-room hotel located within walking distance of the port. It offers free Internet.

WHERE TO EAT

Comme il Faut, Tel Aviv Port, tel: 03 544 6101. This is a very popular restaurant/café, located right on the wooden boardwalk at the port, serving seafood and delicious salads. It is part of a complex of designer shops and a women-only spa, all owned by the same company.
Shalvata, Tel Aviv Port, tel: 03 544 1279, http://shalvata.rest-e.co.il The Shalvata is not only a restaurant and beach bar but also a dance bar by night, right on the water and very family-friendly. Serves tapas, salads, snacks and desserts.

North Tel Aviv at a Glance

Beni Ha-Dayag, Tel Aviv Port, tel: 03 544 0518. This is a famous fish restaurant in the port – the name of the restaurant means 'Benny the Fisherman'. The restaurant is a local institution and you definitely need to book in advance.

Mul Yam, Hangar 24, Tel Aviv Port, tel: 03 546 9920, www.mulyam.com Fabulous gourmet seafood is served at this restaurant, naturally with prices to match. Be sure to book in advance; this is the only restaurant in Israel to be featured in *Les Grandes Tables du Monde*, which ranks it among the 120 finest restaurants in the world.

There are several popular coffee shops located in the area around Basel Square, the north's answer to Neve Tzedek:

Arcafe, 35 Basel Street, tel: 03 546 7001. Arcafe is rated by locals for its delicious pastries; this is a smart deli/coffee shop/patisserie that has several branches in Tel Aviv.

Elkali, 1 Elkali Street, tel: 03 604 1260. This fashionable coffee shop serves all-day snacks and is particularly popular for breakfast.

Lulu, 5 Elkali Street, tel: 03 602 0805. This is another fun place to hang out around the Basel Square area, aimed more at locals than tourists.

There's great shopping at the port, especially for younger tastes. Some of the stores are housed in huge aircraft-style hangars, selling sports gear, trainers and jeans. The northern reaches of the city are also within very easy reach of the centre, around Dizengoff Centre and to Carmel Market, slightly further south. There's a big shopping mall at the Azrieli Towers, where you can get all the big brand names. For a more local feel, you can wander around the atmospheric Basel Square, where there are a lot of small designer shops, gift shops and attractive cafés for breakfast or lunch. Del-Arte on Ashturi Haparchi Street sells handmade items crafted by local artists and designers.

Panoramic **tours of the city** in open-top buses are run by **Dan**, tel: 03 639 4444, www.dan.co.il You can get on and off at any one of the 28 stops and then reboard the bus. The whole tour takes around two hours and commentary is available in eight languages.

Sandemans Tours offers free guided walking tours in Tel Aviv in summer. The idea is that there is no charge for the tour itself and that the guides then earn their money from tips. For more information, visit www.newtelavivtours.com

Tel Aviv Performing Arts Centre: Free backstage tours on Fridays at 11:00 (meet in the foyer) and behind-the-scenes tours on some performance nights, during which you get to see the stage and set and the performers' dressing rooms. Reserve your place in advance on tel: 03 692 7777, www.israel-opera.co.il

Tel Aviv Museum of Art, tel: 03 607 7020, www.tamuseum.co.il The museum offers lectures, children's activities, classical and jazz music recitals and an impressive range of temporary and permanent exhibitions.

The Association for Tourism Tel Aviv-Jaffa, tel: 03 516 6188, Sun–Thu 09:30–17:30; www.visit-tlv.com

Ben Gurion International Airport, flight information, tel: 03 972 3344.

Tourist Information Offices: Ben Gurion Airport, tel: 03 975 4260; also at 46 Herbert Samuel St, tel: 03 516 6188.

Tel Aviv-Jaffa Municipality, Yitzhak Rabin Square, tel: 03 521 8438.

Ha-Yarkon Park, Rokach Boulevard, Tel Aviv, tel: 03 642 2828. Huge urban park with many attractions, including mini-golf, bike rentals, pony rides, a small zoo, a boating pond and various sports courts.

Local information: visit www.visit-tlv.com

5
Jerusalem Old City

A city of honey-coloured stone basking under a deep blue sky, spilling over the arid **Judean Hills**, Jerusalem is infinitely complex. Fortified, fought over, destroyed, rebuilt and seemingly destined to repeat this pattern throughout history, the **Old City** is the focal point of three faiths, Muslim, Christian and Jewish, all worshipping one God, locked in conflict at the same time, but coexisting in relative harmony amidst the crumbling arches, solid stone churches, mosques and synagogues lining the narrow alleys inside the 400-year-old walls.

Outside the Old City, the situation is different. Modern Jerusalem, a thriving commercial centre, extends far beyond the fortifications, luxury hotels, busy shopping streets and swish residential areas clustered amidst almond, pine and cypress trees, spilling over the hills to the west. East of the Old City rises the **Mount of Olives**, with the Arab village of Et-Tur at its summit. This effectively marks the edge of Jerusalem, although the official municipal boundary is further east, while beyond that, the security barrier separates the city from the Palestinian areas.

Putting political views aside, nobody can fail to be captivated by the Old City. Loosely divided into four quarters, Christian, Jewish, Muslim and Armenian, its tangle of streets conceals the **Via Dolorosa**, believed by Christians to be Jesus' route to his crucifixion; the **Western Wall**, the world's holiest site for Jews; and the gleaming gold **Dome of the Rock**, marking the spot for Muslims where Mohammed is believed to have ascended

DON'T MISS

*** Via Dolorosa: walk in the footsteps of Jesus.
*** The Temple Mount: site of the dazzling Dome of the Rock.
*** The Western Wall: this is the holiest site in the world for Jews.
** The Church of the Holy Sepulchre: visit the heart of the Christian religion.
** The souk or market in the bustling **Arab Quarter**, with its hole-in-the-wall falafel joints.

Opposite: *Jerusalem's Western Wall is the holiest site in the whole world for Jews.*

to heaven. You'll stumble across bustling Arab markets, working archaeological digs, ancient Roman streets and countless museums, each one playing its part in piecing together the history of this amazing place.

THE OLD CITY WALLS ★★★

Jerusalem's walled **Old City** is probably the most important site in Israel. The honey-coloured walls, which snake

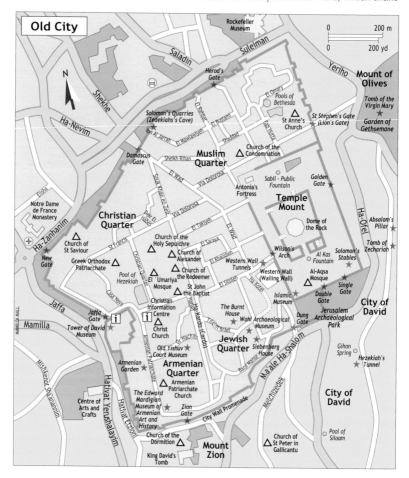

Old City

0   200 m
0   200 yd

Rockefeller Museum

Saladin

Suleiman

N

Yeriho

Mount of Olives

Shekhe

Herod's Gate

El Omary

Tomb of the Virgin Mary

Pools of Bethesda

Ha-Nevim

Solomon's Quarries (Zedekiahs's Cave)

El Rashoo

St Anne's Church

St Stephen's Gate (Lion's Gate)

Garden of Gethsemane

Ibn Al Jarrah

El Mawlawiyeh

Shaddad

El Bustami

Damascus Gate

Sheikh Rihan

Muslim Quarter

Church of the Condemnation

Souk Khan ez-Zeit

El Wad

Via Dolorosa

Sabil - Public Fountain

Golden Gate

Absalom's Pillar

Antonia's Fortress

Notre Dame de France Monastery

Elisha

Deir El Habes

Christian Quarter

Via Dolorosa

Temple Mount

Ha-Ofel

Ha-Zanhanim

St Francis

El Takiyeh

El Saraya

Dome of the Rock

Tomb of Zechariah

Church of St Saviour

Church of the Holy Sepulchre

Church of Alexander

El Khalidieh

Wilson's Arch

Al Kas Fountain

Solomon's Stables

New Gate

Greek Orthodox Patriarchate

Christian Quarter Rd

Church of the Redeemer

Western Wall Tunnels

Western Wall (Wailing Wall)

Al-Aqsa Mosque

Pool of Hezekiah

El Umariya Mosque

St John the Baptist

El Silsileh

Ha-Kotel

Islamic Museum

Double Gate

Single Gate

City of David

Casa Nova

Christian Information Centre

Jaffa

Jaffa Gate

Christ Church

The Burnt House

Wohl Archaeological Museum

Dung Gate

Jerusalem Archaeological Park

Tower of David Museum

Old Yishuv Court Museum

Jewish Quarter

Siebenberg House

Gihon Spring

Mamilla

MAMILLA MALL

Mishkenot Sha'ananim

Armenian Garden

Armenian Patriarchate

Armenian Quarter

Or Hachim (Cardo)

Hativat Ezion

Beyt Israel

Beit Mahse Ha-Shalom

Ma'ale Ha-Shalom

Hezekiah's Tunnel

Centre of Arts and Crafts

The Edward Mardigian Museum of Armenian Art and History

Armenian Patriarchate Church

Zion Gate

City Wall Promenade

Melchizedek

City of David

Hativat Yerushalayim

Church of the Dormition

Mount Zion

Pool of Siloam

King David's Tomb

Church of St Peter in Gallicantu

around the cluster of narrow streets and magnificent churches and temples for over two miles, are remarkably intact considering that they are over 400 years old. The Turkish ruler **Suleiman the Magnificent** was responsible for most of what remains today of the walls, constructed during 1538–41. Other parts date back to the **Crusaders**, and others even further back to King Herod. The walls represent, literally, layer upon layer of history.

There are eight **gates** to the Old City, seven of which are open to people and motor traffic. Belief has it that the eighth, the **Golden Gate** (sealed by the Muslims in the 7th century), will only open on Judgement Day. The gates are all known by their Arab, Jewish and English names. Moving clockwise along the northern wall, the first gate is the **Damascus Gate**, one of the most impressive Islamic buildings around and recently restored. It is open from 09:00–16:00 Monday–Thursday, Saturday and Sunday; 09:00–14:00 Friday. About 100m (328ft) east is **Herod's Gate**, also subject to a recent restoration, where the Crusaders broke through the city walls in July 1099. It was mistakenly believed that Herod's Antipas palace was nearby, hence the gate's name.

St Stephen's Gate, named after the first Christian martyr who was stoned to death here, leads to the Mount of Olives and the Garden of Gethsemane. It's also known as **Lion's Gate**. The **Golden Gate** (the sealed entrance leading to the Temple Mount) is where, according to Christians, the Messiah will enter the city. A Muslim cemetery has been established in front of this gate with a view to hindering the Messiah's progress. The **Dung Gate**, the smallest of the gates, was so named because the area around this gate was once a rubbish dump! Parts of the **Zion Gate** had to be pulled down to give access to a Franciscan monastery that hadn't been incorporated within the city's walls.

The **Jaffa Gate** is important as it marked the point of arrival for people travelling from the ancient port of Jaffa. Lastly, the **New Gate** (opened in 1887) was built mainly to give access from the pilgrim hospices to the Christian holy sites of the Old City.

CLIMATE

Jerusalem, sited on a high plateau, is one of Israel's more temperate areas. Between March and November the weather is usually sunny and pleasant, with average highs of 29°C (86°F) in the hottest months, July and August. Humidity is usually low, but bear in mind that most sightseeing in Jerusalem is on foot and these months may be too hot for pounding the streets.

September and October are full of Jewish holidays so many things may shut down. Winter in Jerusalem is quite cold and from December to February frost and even snow are possible. Failing this, average lows of 6°C (43°F) are normal with chilly and misty evenings.

BIBLICAL TREES

Many of the trees you see around Jerusalem are mentioned in the Bible. The book of **Ezekiel** talks of balsam and cedar, while **Genesis** discusses oak, plane and tamarisk. Almonds, olives and pomegranates appear in **Exodus** and apricots in **Song of Solomon**. **Isiah** talks about figs, myrtle, pine and cypress, while the ubiquitous date palm appears in the book of **Numbers**.

Right: *Visit the Tower of David Museum for an overview of Jerusalem's history.*

Tower of David Museum ★★★

Just inside **Jaffa Gate**, opposite the tourist information office, is one of the city's most important museums, the **Tower of David**. It's almost essential to start here if you have not been to Israel or Jerusalem before; the carefully planned multimedia exhibit tells the story of Jerusalem from its very origins, with bas relief models, archaeological exhibits and thoughtfully arranged panels for a quick visit, or audiovisual for a longer, more detailed tour. The museum itself is housed in a series of guard rooms of the old citadel. The views over the Old City from the top of the ramparts are breathtaking. There are son et lumière shows here, too, in the evenings. Open 10:00–16:00 Sunday–Thursday, 10:00–14:00 Saturday; closed Friday. Guided tours in English daily at 11:00. Sound and Light show Monday, Wednesday, Thursday and Saturday at 20:30 and 22:00.

Ramparts Walk ★★★

Walking part of the ramparts surrounding the Old City is a delightful way of looking down on life on either side of the walls. You can start either at the **Tower of David Museum** or from the **Damascus Gate** and wind your way around the massive fortifications, walking along the top. There are amazing views of **Yemin Moshe** and west Jerusalem, several major Old City Christian churches including the **Church of the Dormition**, a rare glimpse inside the cloistered **Armenian Quarter**, the Valley of Hinnom and, on a clear day, vistas as far afield as the **Judean Desert**.

The Damascus Gate section allows walkers to observe the bustle of the **Arab market** below, the green oasis of the **Garden of Gethsemane** and its beautiful churches, the ancient cemetery on the **Mount of Olives**, and the rooftops of the **Muslim Quarter**. The Jaffa Gate path ends near the Dung Gate, and the Damascus Gate path ends at St Stephen's Gate. Nobody is allowed to walk on the wall near Temple Mount. Open 09:00–16:00 Saturday–Thursday; 09:00–14:00 Friday.

THE CHRISTIAN QUARTER ★★★

The Christian Quarter occupies the northwestern corner of the walled city, its focal point the **Church of the Holy Sepulchre**. In the maze of narrow but clean and orderly streets, the best and most popular route to follow is the **Via Dolorosa**, or the Way of the Cross, the route believed by Christians to have been taken by Jesus from the Praetorium, where he was condemned to death, to Calvary, where he was crucified (*see* page 74 for more detail of the route, which also crosses the Muslim Quarter).

Groups of pilgrims move slowly along the narrow road, stopping to pray at each of the 14 stations (the stops Jesus made along the Via Dolorosa), many of them unable to believe that they are actually in Jerusalem, following (symbolically, at least) Jesus' footsteps. The scene is incredibly moving, although it can get extremely crowded. Recent renovations along the Via Dolorosa have created waiting places for groups, where they can wait for the crowds to thin, and the stations are marked by concentric semicircles of stones set into the street. Less spiritual is the rampant commercialism that pervades the area, with the endless tacky souvenir shops and boutiques lining the route.

WHOSE IS JERUSALEM?

Israel calls Jerusalem its capital but the **United Nations** does not recognize this, and most countries that have relations with Israel have an embassy in Tel Aviv and a consulate in Jerusalem. The 1949 Armistice Line, or Green Line, as it's sometimes called, goes straight through the city, skimming the western side of the Old City. East of the line is 'East Jerusalem', the predominantly Arab neighbourhood annexed by Jordan after the 1949 Armistice and held by them until their defeat in the 1967 Six Day War, when Israel reunited the city. Since 1980 Israel has greatly expanded the municipal boundaries of Jerusalem, taking in Arab villages, but also building new Jewish neighbourhoods. The population of the expanded Jerusalem east of the Green Line is now approximately 208,000 Arabs (*Palestinian Central Bureau of Statistics 2008*) and 188,000 Jews (*Israeli Central Bureau of Statistics 2008*). The United Nations and others regard East Jerusalem as 'occupied territory'. A key demand of the Palestinian Authority has been that East Jerusalem should be the capital of an independent Palestinian state – a position that to date has been unacceptable to Israel because East Jerusalem includes the Western Wall, Temple Mount and the Jewish Quarter of the Old City as well as the new Jewish districts.

JESUS CHRIST SUPERSTAR

The name **Jesus** is derived from a Greek version of the Hebrew name Joshua (or Yehoshuah, meaning 'Jehovah is deliverance'). The title **Christ** comes from the Greek word 'Christos', a translation of the Hebrew 'Mashiakh' or 'Messiah'. 'Christ' was used by Jesus' early followers, who regarded him as the promised deliverer of Israel, and later it was included as part of Jesus' proper name by the church, which regards him as the redeemer of all humanity.

JESUS IN JERUSALEM

The city of Jerusalem is inextricably linked with the ministry of Jesus. According to the Bible, he performed miracles at Bethesda and Bethany; he made a triumphant entry into the city on what is now celebrated as Palm Sunday; he held the Last Supper on Mount Zion; he spent the night in the Garden of Gethsemane, where he was arrested; he faced trial and condemnation in the city; he walked his last steps along the Via Dolorosa; died on Calvary; and rose from the dead.

Walking the Via Dolorosa ★★★

Because Jerusalem has so many layers, the Via Dolorosa is unlikely to be the precise path that Jesus walked. The original is probably hidden under 2000 years of subsequent building – or may be somewhere else entirely, depending on your beliefs. However, when the route and surrounding buildings were given a facelift, large slabs of stone were revealed along the way, believed to date back to Roman times. The route actually begins in what is loosely termed the **Muslim Quarter**, just inside Lion's Gate, and the **Stations of the Cross**, the points at which a significant event occurred, are clearly marked, day and night. Guided tours operate daily from the Pilgrim's Reception Plaza opposite the Crusader Church of St Anne. On Fridays at 15:00, monks from the Franciscan church walk the Stations of the Cross in a solemn procession, which anybody can join. You can also, if you wish, carry a cross; large, wooden **cruficixes** are available to pick up at the first station and leave outside the **Church of the Holy Sepulchre** at the end.

The **First Station of the Cross**, where Pontius Pilate sentenced Jesus to death, is in the courtyard of the Umariyah School. The actual setting is believed to have been Herod's **Antonia Fortress**, the foundations now covered by the churches lining the Via Dolorosa. It's also now the exit point of the controversial **Western Wall Tunnels** and is heavily guarded.

The **Second Station**, where Jesus received his cross and a crown of thorns was placed on his head, is op-

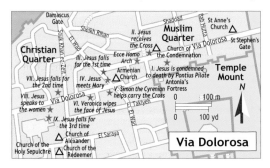

Via Dolorosa

Left: *The Via Dolorosa depicts the last hours of Christ in Jerusalem.*

posite the Franciscan Church of the Condemnation, where there is a beautiful little chapel with intricate designs on its stained-glass windows.

The **Third Station**, marking his first fall, is at the point where Via Dolorosa crosses the street El Wad. The **Fourth Station**, where Jesus encountered his mother, Mary, is marked by an Armenian Church. At the **Fifth Station**, Simon the Cyrenian helped Jesus carry the cross. The **House of St Veronica** marks the **Sixth**, where Veronica wiped Jesus' face with her veil. The Via Dolorosa then bisects the Souk Khan ez-Zeit, the location of the **Seventh Station**, where Jesus fell for the second time.

Two more stations lie outside the Church of the Holy Sepulchre. The **Eighth** is marked by a Greek Orthodox chapel, **St Charalambous**, built over the spot where Jesus spoke to the women of Jerusalem: 'Weep not for me, but for Jerusalem'. A pillar marks the point at which he fell a third time – the **Ninth Station**. The remaining five stations are contained within the Church of the Holy Sepulchre.

Church of the Holy Sepulchre ★★★

The squat Church – or churches, to be precise – of the Holy Sepulchre, the very heart of the Christian Quarter, covers **Calvary** (**Golgotha** in Hebrew), the **Place of the**

GOLGOTHA'S AUTHENTICITY

Is Golgotha the actual spot where Jesus died? There are arguments for its authenticity.
• The geography matches the Gospel descriptions: a rock that looked like a skull outside the city (John 19:17) with a grave nearby (John 19:41–2).
• Very early Christians worshipped here until AD66 (according to historians Eusebius and Socrates Scholasticus).
• Even when the area was incorporated into the city walls in AD41–43 it was left untouched. Why?
• The Roman Emperor Hadrian built a Temple of Venus over the site in AD135.
• Constantine tore down Hadrian's temple in AD326 to build his own church, despite the availability of a better site nearby.
• The eyewitness historian Eusebius claimed that in the course of the excavations, the original memorial was discovered.

THE TRUE CROSS

It is believed that St Helena, Constantine's mother, discovered (during excavations to build Constantine's church) the actual cross on which Jesus was crucified, near the tomb. There were three crosses: those of the two thieves and that of Christ. Legend has it that to establish which one belonged to Christ, a sick man was brought to touch each cross, and he was miraculously healed by one of them.

In the small **Chapel of the Finding of the Cross**, there is an altar featuring a life-sized statue of St Helena holding a cross. This side of the chapel is owned by the Catholic Church, with the Greek Orthodox Church owning the other side.

Skull, where Jesus is believed to have died on the cross. Much of the present structure dates from around the 12th century and was built by the Crusaders, although a place of worship has stood in this location since the 4th century.

The Holy Sepulchre is actually a cluster of five churches, some with a bigger part of the communal space than others. For first-time (and secular) visitors, it's difficult to distinguish between **Armenian** and **Greek Orthodox**, **Syrian Orthodox**, **Roman Catholic** and **Abyssinian Coptic**, and there's always a service going on somewhere in the maze, chanting in different languages, the air heavy with incense and bearded priests scuttling backwards and forwards in the dim light. Thousands of pilgrims flock here and it is almost always busy, with queues to access the five Stations of the Cross.

The **Church of Calvary** is especially beautiful, with a stunning **mosaic** on one wall depicting the Stations of the Cross. The Greek Orthodox Church is extremely wealthy, abundant with silver and gold artefacts. The **Ethiopian church**, however, is one of the most touching – it is very small, dark and simple, and is tended by a lone monk.

Crowds of tourists are bound to visit the remaining five stations in slow-moving lines. To grasp the significance of each area, a professional guide is a good idea.

Inside the door, up a flight of steep steps (deliberately made so, so that pilgrims could empathize with the suffering of Jesus), is **Golgotha** and the **Tenth Station**, where Jesus was stripped. A mosaic in the floor tells the story. The next three stations, located close together and marked by altars, attract large crowds. Here Jesus was nailed to the cross, the cross was hoisted upright, and his body was later taken down. The final, 14th Station is the **Holy**

Sepulchre itself. The marble tomb below contains the rock that guarded the entrance, the burial site, and the tomb of **Joseph of Arimathea**. There are long queues to walk past the tomb but having come this far, it is worth it: small, dark, atmospheric, lit by candles. Open 05:00–20:00 daily Apr–Sep and 05:00–19:00 daily Oct–Mar. Early morning can be an especially beautiful and peaceful time to come.

Opposite: *Riches in the gloom of the interior of the cavernous Church of the Holy Sepulchre.*

THE JEWISH QUARTER ★★★

The Jewish Quarter is perhaps the most atmospheric part of the old city and has been subject to an incredibly turbulent history, having been destroyed in 1948, ruled by the Jordanians for 19 years and rebuilt in 1967 when Jerusalem was reunified. Like the rest of the city, it comprises layer upon layer of building, hidden archways leading to ancient staircases and tiny, dark alleyways, the scent of summer jasmine heavy in the air after sunset. The most spectacular and holy site is the **Western Wall**, the most important place in the world to Jews and also of enormous significance to Christians and Muslims.

The Cardo ★★

Walk along the Cardo, a fascinating Roman street, laid down in the 6th century as the city's main thoroughfare. At various points, you can look down through glass sections at the ancient cobbled road and the remnants of arches and buildings from 1400 years ago. There are elements of Ottoman, Crusader and Byzantine architecture, the oldest sections of the excavations below the street dating back to the 8th century BC. Lines of bricks laid into the stone underfoot indicate the outline of former streets – orange bricks depict a street from the 8th century BC and black bricks the 1st century BC.

Alone on the Walls Museum ★

This tiny photographic exhibit tells the story of the fall of the Jewish Quarter in 1948, as recorded by the American **John Philips**, a photojournalist who was in Jerusalem for the whole battle as a correspondent for *Life Magazine*.

> ### OCCUPATION OF THE JEWISH QUARTER
>
> Between 1948 and 1967, the Jewish Quarter of Jerusalem was in ruins, having been invaded by an Arab Legion force. There were 1600 inhabitants of the quarter at the time, defended by just 150 soldiers. Some 69 casualties were suffered by the Jews and heavy damage was sustained by the old buildings. After the fall of the quarter and the declaration of surrender, some residents were allowed out through the Zion Gate, while others were taken to a prisoner of war camp in Jordan. Looters worked their way through the quarter and then set fire to it. In 1967, after reunification of the area, renovation work began.

JOIN A DIG

Would-be archaeologists can volunteer to join a dig in Israel. You'll need to pay for your own travel and accommodation, although some digs arrange simple rooms in hostels or kibbutzim. No experience is necessary, although you do need to go through an application process. The work is often hot and tedious but can be enormously satisfying; many digs will start before dawn and stop at noon, with the afternoon devoted to lectures or cleaning and examining the morning's finds. There's a list of current digs on the Ministry of Foreign Affairs website (www.mfa.gov.il).

Philips actually joined the Arab Legion on 19 May 1948, dressed as a Legionnaire, and moved around the area under cover. When the Jewish Quarter of Jerusalem fell on 29 May, Philips recorded the dramatic scenes. Beautifully shot, the images are both graphic and moving. The museum was opened on the 40th anniversary of the liberation of Jerusalem, in 2007. Open 09:00–17:00 Sunday–Thursday; 09:00–13:00 Friday.

Wohl Archaeological Museum ★

This is a fascinating archaeological site in Hakara'im Street, giving a clear insight into the lives of Jerusalem's nobility during the **Second Temple Period**. The site comprises six houses, discovered when the Jewish Quarter was being renovated in 1967, with three of them on display. Beautiful mosaics and frescoes were found and you'll see all sorts of other signs of great wealth: storage rooms, reservoirs for water, ritual baths, stoneware for serving food, terracotta tableware, amphorae that would have contained wine, and delicate flasks. The rooms were spacious, some with balconies, and archaeologists have confirmed that the buildings would have been two storeys high. Open 09:00–17:00 Sunday–Thursday; 09:00–13:00 Friday.

Below: *The Wohl Archaeological Museum gives an insight into life during the Second Temple Period.*

Western Wall ★★★

The Western Wall, or the **Kotel**, is the holiest site in the whole of Jerusalem to Jews, as it is the last remnant of

the Temple that housed the **Ark of the Covenant**. The plaza in front of the remaining exposed section of the wall is one of the city's most famous sights, divided into a men's and a women's area, where Jews from all over the world come to pray.

Visitors can go up to the wall, although you must be appropriately dressed. It is best to avoid Friday afternoons, when a lot of Orthodox Jews come to pray, many of whom do not appreciate the attention of tourists, and cameras should be used with great discretion. Monday is a good day to visit, when a lot of **Bar Mitzvahs** take place and you may see long processions, some with musical accompaniment, and large groups dressed in white to celebrate the occasion. It is customary to place your prayer to God on a piece of paper and slip it between the ancient stones. You'll see religious people nodding repetitively, reading prayers and, sometimes, weeping. It is a profoundly moving occasion. Open 24 hours a day.

Western Wall Tunnels ★★★

This amazing piece of excavation extends the entire 488m (1600ft) of the Wall, underground, deep below the modern city, revealing stonework from **Herod's** time. You'll pass ancient **cisterns**, water courses and **quarries** and, at one point, a tiny section of the Wall itself, usually occupied with four or five women praying (this section allows them to get closer to the holiest part of the wall than the women's section of the exposed area in the Plaza). During the walk through the narrow tunnels, you can appreciate the enormous scale of the excavation, with sudden drop-offs down through even more layers of history or glances up through the stone ceiling to vast, hidden caverns. The tunnels start at the Western Wall Plaza and emerge on Lion's Gate Road by a Muslim school. Visits take place in groups (you should book well in advance on tel: 1 599 515888, www.thekotel.org). Don't visit the Western Wall Tunnels if you are claustrophobic or heavily overweight – the tunnels are extremely narrow and you may encounter groups coming the other way. It's hot, too. Open from 07:00 till evening, depending on bookings, Sunday–Thursday; 07:00–12:00 Friday.

The Burnt House ★

Would-be archaeologists should call in at the Burnt House on Tiferet Street, where there's a fascinating audiovisual show of the excavations of the Jewish Quarter. This luxurious house belonged to a religious

THE BAR MITZVAH

Bar Mitzvah (or Bat Mitzvah for girls) literally means 'son (or daughter) of the commandment' and is the coming-of-age ceremony for Jewish boys at the age of 13 and girls at the age of 12, after which they become obliged to observe the commandments. The ceremony is actually a modern phenomenon, not mentioned in the Talmud and rarely practised until 100 years or so ago. Typically, the celebrant will study for a year or more in advance and on the big day give a *drasha* (a short sermon) and chant from the Torah scroll and from the Haftarah (extracts from the prophets) during the synagogue service. The religious service is followed by an elaborate party, often as elaborate as a wedding, during which the celebrant makes a speech.

GATEWAY TO THE PAST

The restored and reopened southern side of Temple Mount – the rebuilt Hulda Steps, the Jerusalem Archaeological Park and Davidson Centre – has been included in Chapter 6 (*see* pages 89–90). The entrance to these sites is alongside Western Wall Plaza and just inside the Old City walls at Dung Gate.

family called **Kathros** in the Second Temple Period (538BC–AD70, after the Jewish exiles had returned from Babylon and rebuilt the Temple) but was burnt by the Romans in AD70 along with the rest of Jerusalem, only to be discovered 1900 years later. Its sooty remains are better preserved than many of the other buildings and it has been converted into a museum, although a residential house has been built over the ancient remains.

The Kathros family, who are referred to in the **Talmud**, were powerful and affluent priests. The residence included a courtyard, several living rooms, a kitchen and a bath, although only the basement survived the fire. Several stone tools and dishes, some engraved, and the sword of a **Roman soldier**, were found here. It is open Sunday 10:00–17:00; Mon–Thu 09:00–17:00; Fri 09:00–13:00.

THE MUSLIM QUARTER ★★★

The northeastern sector of the city, bordering the Temple Mount, is the Muslim Quarter, busy and bustling, with a colourful, noisy market (souk) selling everything from fruit and vegetables to brassware, household goods, fragrances, fabrics and souvenirs.

Below: *Arab markets inside the Old City are a constant source of noise and colour.*

St Anne's Church and the Bethesda Pools ★★

Just inside the **Lion's Gate**, before the start of the Via Dolorosa and hidden amidst lush gardens behind a wooden door, is **St Anne's**, a beautiful 12th-century church dedicated to Anne, or Hannah, the mother of Mary. It's a Christian church, despite being in the Muslim area of the city. The solid-looking church was built between 1131 and 1138 by the **Crusaders**, and much of what you see today is original. What's special about the church is its wonderful

acoustics; visiting choirs book months in advance to come and sing here and the sound of soaring voices often accompanies any visit to the church grounds. In the grounds are the **Bethesda Pools**, where Jesus is believed to have healed the cripple, according to the book of St John. The pools were also formerly a huge and impressive reservoir, today crumbling and overgrown but still a focal point of the city for visiting pilgrims. Open 08:00–12:00 and 14:00–18:00 Monday–Saturday; closed Sunday.

Temple Mount ★★★

The Temple Mount, site of the Jewish Temple, is also sacred to Muslims as it is believed to be the site from which **Mohammed the Prophet** ascended to heaven. The **Dome of the Rock**, that magnificent gold dome that is so prominent on the Jerusalem skyline, is built over the spot where Abraham is believed to have prepared his son, Isaac, for sacrifice (Abraham is also an important historical figure in Muslim belief). Muslims pay homage to a small enclosure where there's a footprint of Mohammed, and some hairs from his beard. There is also a handprint, believed to be of the **Archangel Gabriel**, who held down the rock as Mohammed ascended. The silver-coloured **Al-Aqsa Mosque**, built to commemorate the furthest point Mohammed travelled from Mecca, is the third most holy site to Muslims after Mecca and Medina. Non-Muslims are not allowed inside the mosque but are welcome on tours of the compound, which features many superb examples of Islamic art and architecture, minarets, tiles and artwork. Open Sunday–Thursday 07:30–10:00 and 12:30–13:30. Closed on religious holidays and 'sensitive' days. Bring your passport as ID. The Temple Mount is closed on all Christian, Jewish or Muslim holidays and any other days considered 'sensitive' by the Muslim custodians of the site. Many Jews do not wish to come here for fear of treading on a sacred part of the Temple.

Above: *The Bethesda Pools were a remarkable architectural achievement for their time.*

THE ARMENIAN QUARTER

In the quiet, almost private southwestern quarter of the Old City, the Armenian community keeps to itself, with its own food, customs and Orthodox beliefs. You can look down on the narrow streets from the ramparts walk or wander through them, looking into the huge **Armenian Patriarchate Church**, rich with art and ritual artefacts.

Jerusalem Old City at a Glance

BEST TIMES TO VISIT

March to May and late September to October are the best times to visit Jerusalem as the heat is less intense. For detailed tours of the Old City, winter can be a great time as there are hardly any crowds. The weather can be damp and drizzly or, if you're lucky, dazzlingly clear, but take warm clothes either way from November to February. In the middle of summer, visit the Old City early in the morning or late in the evening to avoid both the crowds and the heat. If you are travelling in September, check the dates of Jewish holidays as many attractions will be closed at odd hours during this time.

GETTING THERE

The closest airport to Jerusalem is **Tel Aviv's Ben Gurion International Airport**, about 40 minutes from the city by taxi or *sherut*: try **Nesher Taxis Sherut**, tel: 02 625 7227. There are regular Egged **bus** services from Tel Aviv (www.egged.co.il) and also from other parts of the country, as well as **trains** from Tel Aviv (www.rail.co.il). You can **rent a car** at Ben Gurion International Airport, but there is little point if your only destination is Jerusalem, as traffic is pretty bad in the city, not to mention parking (or lack thereof). **Public transport** is best for getting to Jerusalem, and walking is best for getting around.

GETTING AROUND

The way to get around the largely pedestrianized Old City is on foot, through the narrow alleyways and up and down many steps. There are guided tours for every possible interest (Christian or Jewish, for example), or you can get a map from the tourist information office at the Jaffa Gate and find your own way around. If you're in a wheelchair or have trouble walking, visit www.accessinisrael.org which has step-free routes around the Old City and also useful information about accessible areas inside the main attractions.

WHERE TO STAY

Almost all hotels in Jerusalem are outside the walls of the Old City, although there are a few hostels within the ramparts. Staying here is very special; you'll get a completely different view of the city.

MID-RANGE

Austrian Hospice of the Holy Family, 37 Via Dolorosa, PO Box 19600, 91194 Jerusalem, tel: 02 626 5800, www.austrianhospice.com Simple but comfortable rooms with private facilities as well as dormitories. Austrian café serving great *sachertorte* with whipped cream, apple strudel, goulash soup and Wiener schnitzel with potato salad.

BUDGET

New Swedish Hostel, David St, 29 Jaffa Gate, PO Box 19084, Jerusalem. Basic hostel in the heart of the bazaar of the old city, two minutes from Jaffa Gate and the Church of the Holy Sepulchre.

Jaffa Gate Hostel, Jaffa Gate, in front of David's Tower, 19383 Jerusalem. Welcoming hostel with its own tours, free Wi-Fi, and movies and *nargelas* (water pipes) to hire. Dorms or private rooms with showers.

Agron Guest House, Agron 6, tel: 02 594 5522, www.iyha.org.il 55 rooms and two restaurants, within walking distance of the sights of the Old City.

WHERE TO EAT

The Old City isn't really a popular or convenient place to come for dinner; there simply isn't the space or access for a large restaurant here. There are, however, plenty of excellent hole-in-the-wall falafel joints and snack places for fast food, Israeli-style, at lunchtime.

Coffee Shop, Jaffa Gate, tel: 02 628 6812. Pleasant spot for a hearty lunch of soup and salad. Turn right after David's Tower inside the Jaffa Gate.
The Austrian Hospice, 37 Via Dolorosa, tel: 02 626 5800, www.austrianhospice.com Wiener schnitzel in the heart of the Old City in an elegant Viennese coffee house that is also a hostel for pilgrims.
Abu Shukri, 63 El Wad Rd, tel: 02 627 1538. One of the

Jerusalem Old City at a Glance

Old City's most famous falafel joints, very basic, selling falafel in pittas, dollops of hummus, beans and salads, perfect for a quick lunch on the run.

Jafar Sweets, 42 Souk Khan ez-Zeit, Old City (enter from Damascus Gate and swerve right when the street forks into Via Dolorosa).

Bonkers Bagels, 5 Tiferet Israel St, Jewish Quarter, tel: 02 628 0081. Tiny café/shop selling nothing but bagels, with a variety of toppings.

Armenian Tavern, 79 Armenian Orthodox Patriarchate Road, tel: 02 627 3854. Authentic Armenian atmosphere with music, mosaics, a splashing fountain and the surroundings of a former Crusader church. Armenian specialities are served here – grilled meats and spicy sausages – and also pizza.

SHOPPING

Much of the Old City is taken up with market stalls, particularly in the **Muslim Quarter**, where you'll find olivewood chess and nativity sets, rosaries, wooden camels, glassware from Hebron, mother-of-pearl objects, silver jewellery and a variety of leather goods. You will also see Bedouin weavings and rugs of varying quality. There are further stalls selling fragrant spices, oils, potions, sticky baklava cakes and fake designer bags, suitcases and

designer clothes. You're expected to haggle hard for everything you wish to buy. Some of the nicer shops sell tasteful (and comical) Judaica, from menorahs to Western Wall fridge magnets.

The shops along the Cardo are more glitzy, with expensive designer jewellery, high-class Judaica, antiques and art galleries. Try **Bar-On Jewish Art and Antiquities** or **Rozen Jewellers**.

TOURS AND EXCURSIONS

If you are visiting Jerusalem under your own steam, it's a good idea to book a private tour guide; all guides registered with the tourist board are listed, with the languages they speak, on www.goisrael.com

The **Municipality of Jerusalem** offers free walking tours with qualified guides. Meet by the palm trees on Safra Square at 10:00 daily; tel: 02 531 4600 for times and dates, as there's a huge variety of tours. Other free tours of the Old City are offered by **Sandemans New Europe Tours Ltd**, daily at 11:00, departing from the tourist information point at the Jaffa Gate. The guides wear

red T-shirts. You're expected to tip them, as the 3.5-hour tours are free. Guided tours are offered by numerous operators. Try **Jerusalem Experience**, tel: 077 558 6001, www.jerusalem experience.co.il for small group tours (up to six) with different themes – Jewish, Three Religions, King David, for example. Or book a private tour guide: tel: 03 751 1132, or visit http://itga.org.il/english For tours through the Western Wall Tunnels, you have to book in advance: tel: 02 627 1333, www.thekotel.org

USEFUL CONTACTS

Tourist Information Centre Ministry of Tourism, Jaffa Gate, tel: 02 627 1422.
Police, 1 Saladin St, tel: 02 626 1378.
Lost Credit Card Lines: AmEx, tel: 1 800 940 3211; MC, tel: 1 800 941 8873.
Christian Information Centre, Jaffa Gate, PO Box 14308, Jerusalem 91142, tel: 02 627 2692, fax: 02 628 6417, www.cicts.org
Jaffa Gate, PO Box 14308, Jerusalem 91142.

JERUSALEM	J	F	M	A	M	J	J	A	S	O	N	D
AVERAGE TEMP °C	9	9	13	16	20	23	24	25	23	21	16	11
AVERAGE TEMP °F	48	48	55	61	68	73	75	77	73	70	61	52
RAINFALL mm	132	132	64	28	3	0	0	0	0	13	71	86
RAINFALL in	5.2	5.2	2.5	1.09	0.11	0	0	0	0	0.51	2.8	3.4
DAYS OF RAINFALL	18	18	12	5	2	0	0	0	0	3	12	14

6. Eastern Jerusalem and Around the Walls

In terms of Jerusalem's centuries of history, the Old City is relatively new and there are many more ancient treasures to be explored outside its massive stone walls. Spend a day sifting through the very beginnings of Jerusalem at the fascinating **City of David**, the original settlement southeast of the walls, now a working archaeological dig, or explore the **Archaeological Park**, much of what's been uncovered dating back to the Second Temple Period. Explore the **caves** and **tombs** under and around the Old City, revealing ancient water systems that sustained the residents in times of siege; you can evoke the mood by bringing a torch and wading through the old water channel of **Hezekiah's Tunnel**, dating back to 701 BC.

No visit to Jerusalem is complete without standing on the **Mount of Olives** and contemplating that breathtaking vista of the Old City laid out before you, the golden **Dome of the Rock** gleaming like a beacon of faith in the sunshine, the stone walls snaking around the jumble of houses, alleys and places of worship within. Spend a moment in the beautiful **Garden of Gethsemane** or walk up to the Russian Orthodox **Church of Mary Magdalene** with its shimmering gold onion domes. You can also explore the ancient **cemeteries** on the Mount of Olives and **Mount Zion** – Catholic, Jewish and Muslim – and identify the graves of people who have shaped the history of Israel and asked to spend eternity buried in this most spiritual of places.

Opposite: *Head for the Mount of Olives for the finest views across Jerusalem's Old City.*

The Mount of Olives ★★★

The Mount of Olives, rising up behind the Old City in East Jerusalem, is the best place to go for spectacular views. Sunrise and sunset are the most beautiful times. It's from here that you can see the spectacular view of the golden **Dome of the Rock** with the Old City spread out behind it.

The olive-less hill is steeped in legend and belief. The **Jewish cemetery**, still in use, dates back to biblical times and is considered the most sacred in the world. Jesus is believed to have entered Jerusalem from the Mount of Olives, through the Golden Gate, which is now sealed until the arrival of the next Messiah. Jews and Christians believe that a Messiah will resurrect the dead and lead them once again through the gate, so the Mount of Olives is in great demand as a burial site. Muslims also believe that the dead will rise here on the **Day of Judgement** and the section below the city walls is the Muslim cemetery.

Dome of the Ascension ★

The rocky slopes of the Mount of Olives are dotted with churches, some spectacular, some modest. The small

Dome of the Ascension marks the spot from which Jesus is believed to have ascended to heaven. There has been a church here since AD390, later a Crusader church and still later, from the 17th century, a mosque and minaret were added.

The site is of significance because of the presence of a slab of rock believed to bear the footprint of Jesus (Jesus' ascension is recognized by Islam, although the

Left: *The Church of All Nations is designed in the Byzantine style.*
Opposite: *The Dome of the Ascension marks the spot from where Jesus is believed to have ascended to heaven.*

event does not appear in the Qur'an). Open 08:00–18:00 daily; closes at 16:30 in winter.

On the path that leads down to the city, the walls of the **Pater Noster Carmelite Convent** are decorated with the Lord's Prayer.

Church of Mary Magdalene ★★

One of the city's most beautiful churches, with its seven golden domes, this **Russian Orthodox** church was built in 1888 by Tsar Alexander III. The crypt holds the remains of the tsar's mother, the Grand Duchess Elizabeth, who was killed in the Russian revolution of 1917. Also buried here is **Princess Alice of Greece** (the mother-in-law of Britain's Queen Elizabeth II), who provided sanctuary for Jews during the Nazi occupation of Greece in World War II.

Inside the church there are beautiful wall paintings and sumptuous icons in gold and jewel-like colours, typical of the Russian Orthodox style. Open Tuesday and Thursday, 10:00–12:00.

Church of All Nations ★★

The contemporary Church of All Nations stands at the foot of the Mount of Olives, next to the peaceful **Garden of Gethsemane**. The church, also known as the

---

THE INN OF THE GOOD SAMARITAN

The Parable of the Good Samaritan in the Gospel of Luke tells of the wounded Jew who was ignored by other travellers, most of them Samaritans, once sworn enemies of the Jews. However, one Samaritan stopped to help the traveller and took him to an inn. Although the story is fiction, a sign marks the spot, some 10km (6 miles) from the Mount of Olives on the Jericho Road, where the inn was supposed to have been. As travellers' inns were commonplace in the 1st century, the likelihood of some kind of building having existed here is strong.

Basilica of the Agony, was built between 1919 and 1924. It was funded by 12 countries, hence the reference to 'All Nations'. It was designed by **Antonio Barluzzi** in a Byzantine style, with sturdy pillars, a domed roof and floor mosaics, and has a dazzling and powerful mosaic on the façade depicting Jesus as a link between man and God. Inside, the symbols of the countries that built the church are inlaid in the ceilings of the 12 gold cupolas. The church is run by Franciscans (Catholic) but has an Anglican service in the garden on Maundy Thursday, the day before Good Friday. Open Monday–Saturday, 08:00–12:00 and 14:00–17:30.

Above: *The Garden of Gethsemane is a quiet place for contemplation.*
Opposite: *Much of what you'll see in the Jerusalem Archaeological Park dates back to the Second Temple Period.*

Garden of Gethsemane ★

Next to the Church of All Nations, at the foot of the hill, is the Garden of Gethsemane, where Jesus was betrayed and arrested. The gnarled olive trees in the garden are believed to be up to 2000 years old, although they are unlikely to be from the exact time of Christ as the Romans are believed to have destroyed all the olive trees around Jerusalem during the **siege of AD70**. The trees are, nonetheless, impressively ancient and the garden is a peaceful place for quiet contemplation. It is open daily from 08:30–11:30 and 14:30–16:00.

Tomb of the Virgin Mary ★

A path to the left of the garden leads underground to the candlelit tombs of the Virgin Mary's parents, **Anne** and **Joachim**. Some believe the 5th-century chapel also contains the remains of Mary herself and her husband,

Joseph, although the Bible provides no accurate account of the end of Mary's life or the place of her burial. Open daily 06:00–11:45 and 14:30–17:00.

Church of Dominus Flevit ★

This is another modern church, shaped by architect **Antonio Barluzzi** as a tear drop, commemorating the spot where, according to the Bible, Jesus approached Jerusalem and wept as he predicted that the city would be 'dashed to the ground' (which it was, in AD70). The church is built over earlier remains and some ancient tombs. There's a breathtaking view of the **Temple Mount** through one of the windows. Open daily 08:00–12:00 and 14:30–17:00.

Jerusalem Archaeological Park ★★

The Jerusalem Archaeological Park is an archaeological dig and open-air museum stretching from the **Temple Mount** in the north, the slope of the Mount of Olives and the Kidron Valley in the east and the **Valley of Hinnom** to the west and the south. Much of what you can see dates back to the Second Temple Period; at one

CONQUESTS OF ALLENBY

War hero Viscount Allenby (1861–1936) was born in Felixstowe, England, and educated at the Royal Military Academy, Sandhurst. Allenby was assigned in 1917 as commander-in-chief of the Egyptian Expeditionary Force. He led an offensive against the Turkish armies in the Middle East, capturing Jerusalem on 9 December 1917, winning decisively at Megiddo in September 1918, and taking Damascus on 1 October 1918. The campaign forced the Turks to retreat, and Allenby was promoted to the rank of field marshal. From 1919–25 he was British high commissioner in Egypt. The main Israel-Jordan border crossing, the Allenby Bridge, is named after him.

point, there is a pile of huge stones, fallen from the Western Wall, and a direct result of the destruction of the Second Temple. There is also a staircase located south of the Temple Mount, leading to the **Double (Hulda) Gate**, and a series of stone-cut channels connecting the area with the Temple Mount. Ritual baths (*miqva'ot*) and cisterns were uncovered throughout the area, as well as a **Herodian** street.

Also in the park is the **Davidson Centre**, an audiovisual display in a recently excavated underground storage complex belonging to a 7th-century Umayyad Palace. Visitors can see a fascinating audiovisual reconstruction of the **Herodian Temple Mount** as it was in AD70, prior to the destruction of the Second Temple by the Romans. Open Sunday–Thursday 08:00–17:00 and Friday 08:00–14:00.

City of David ★★

Outside the Dung Gate of the Old City is a fascinating archaeological dig, now a major visitor attraction, slowly uncovering the City of David on and under the slopes of the Kidron Valley.

The excavation of the City of David is uncovering secrets from more than 3000 years ago, when King David left the city of Hebron for a small hilltop settlement known as Jerusalem, establishing it as the unified capital of the tribes of Israel. The City of David extended down the hill southwards from what is now **Temple Mount**. Its location was of strategic importance, surrounded by valleys on three sides, providing natural protection, and also conveniently on top of the **Gihon Spring**, one of the biggest water sources in the Judean Hills and later to become the main water source for Jerusalem for over 1000 years.

It was David's son, **King Solomon**, who built the First Temple on top of Mount Moriah, now better known as Temple Mount.

This is a fascinating visit for all ages. Much of the interactive one-hour tour is underground, visiting some of the newest archaeological excavations at the site –

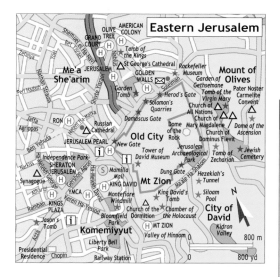

Eastern Jerusalem

fortresses and tunnels buried beneath millennia of history. You'll see the impressive shaft discovered in 1867 by the archaeologist **Charles Warren**, through which the people of the city drew water from the spring. The underground part of the tour ends at the Gihon Spring where, according to the Book of Kings in the Bible, Solomon was anointed king.

Part of the site is **Hezekiah's Tunnel**, an optional extension to the tour. In 701BC, Hezekiah, king of Judah, designed an ingenious tunnel connecting the Gihon Spring, the city's only water supply, from outside the city to within the walls, creating the **Siloam Pool** and so preventing having the water source cut off by the enemy. Workmen dug from both ends, zigzagging under the city until they met in the middle.

The 500m (550yd) Hezekiah's Tunnel is a highlight for many now. Visitors can trudge through the wet tunnel, holding a torch, a walk that takes about 40 minutes.

There are other activities at the site. You can walk through the 2000-year-old **Armon Hanatziv Aqueduct**, which used to bring water from **Solomon's Pools** near Bethlehem to the Temple. This tour takes an hour and a

GATEWAYS TO THE OLD CITY

There are a number of entrances to the Old City, all of them subject to ongoing preservation efforts. **Herod's Gate** leads to the Muslim Quarter from the north, while the magnificent **Damascus Gate**, also on the northern wall, is one of the busiest. **New Gate**, only built in 1889, leads to the Christian Quarter. The largest entrance and the busiest is **Jaffa Gate**, on the west side next to the Citadel. **Zion Gate** in the south, opening into the Jewish Quarter, is the entrance through which IDF soldiers entered in 1967 to capture the Old City – you can still see the bullet marks. **Dung Gate** got its name as it used to be the exit point for refuse from the city. On the eastern side, **Lion's Gate**, the most likely entrance for pilgrims, leads to the Via Dolorosa. The **Triple Gate**, **Double Gate** and **Single Gate** are all sealed, while from the Mount of Olives you can see the outline of the **Golden Gate**, which was constructed in the post-Byzantine Period. Jews believe that the Messiah will enter the city through this gate, so the Muslims under Suleiman sealed it as a preventative measure.

half and you need a torch (they're for sale at the site); it's not recommended if you're claustrophobic. There are four-wheel-drive buggy tours of the Mount of Olives and, for children, sessions helping the archaeologists to sift through the rubble, looking for small treasures.

Ancient meets modern in the **Segway Tour**, using 'human transporters' (two-wheeled, gyroscopically controlled devices) to drive along some of the promenades overlooking Jerusalem.

The site is open 08:00–19:00 Sunday–Wednesday; until 22:00 on Thursdays for night-time tours; 08:00–15:00 Friday (in winter it is open 08:00–17:00 Sunday–Thursday and 08:00–13:00 Friday).

The Garden Tomb ★

Some Anglicans believe that the 'real' Golgotha lies outside the current city walls. The Garden Tomb, reached through the **Damascus Gate** on the alley of Conrad Schick Street, does match the biblical description, although it is not officially recognized by the church. True, the hill beside it is shaped like a skull and

Below: *The Damascus Gate is one of the entrances to the Old City, set in the solid ramparts.*

the rock-hewn cavern is typical of the time, but the tomb itself dates back to the 7th century BC, whereas the Bible describes Jesus' tomb as 'new', and it was disfigured a few hundred years later in the **Byzantine** Period, indicated that early Christians did not regard it as a special place. The tomb was discovered in 1883 by **General Charles Gordon**.

Today, it is maintained by the British Garden Tomb Association, the entrance overlooking an English country garden. Open Monday–Saturday 08:30–12:00 and 14:00–17:30.

Rockefeller Museum ★

Close to the Garden Tomb, the Rockefeller Museum on Sultan Suleiman Street houses an interesting display of archaeological finds discovered during the **British Mandate** Period, from 1920 to 1948. The museum was established by the British and funded by American philanthropist John D Rockefeller.

The exhibits are displayed in chronological order, from two million years ago to AD1700. Among the museum's most famous possessions are 8th-century wooden panels from Al-Aqsa Mosque and 12th-century marble lintels from the Church of the Holy Sepulchre. The museum is open 10:00–15:00 Sunday–Thursday; 10:00–14:00 Friday and Saturday.

Zedekiah's Cave ★

There's more underground exploration to be had on the north side of the Old City, between Damascus Gate and Herod's Gate, in Zedekiah's Cave, also known as **Solomon's Quarries**. This vast underground cavern could have been the source of stone for Solomon's Temple. Some people believe that the caves lead all the way to Jericho; King Zedekiah was supposed to have fled from the Babylonians through the caves in 587BC and is said to have been captured somewhere near Jericho. You can explore the caves 09:00–16:00 Monday–Thursday and Saturday, and 09:00–14:00 Friday.

WILD BEASTS

Israel has an impressive 116 different species of land animals, compared with 140 species in the whole of Europe, which is 300 times larger. The largest land animals are the mountain gazelles, wild boar, foxes, jungle cats, Nubian ibex and the rarely seen leopards, hyenas, jackals and wolves. Almost all of these, however, are endangered.

Since the 1960s, the **Nature Reserves Authority** has been reintroducing populations of animals which were native to the area 2000 years ago, under a programme known as **Hai-Bar**. There are breeding centres in the Carmel region and Arava, in the desert, aimed at increasing the population of ostriches, roe deer, Asiatic wild asses, Persian fallow deer and white oryx. The Asiatic wild ass, fallow deer and white oryx have already been successfully reintroduced into the wild.

OSKAR SCHINDLER

Entrepreneur Oskar Schindler, a German, acquired and ran a factory in Poland during World War II, producing enamel goods and munitions to supply the German front. Although he hobnobbed with the Gestapo, he allowed Jews to invest in the factory and paid off the Nazis so that these Jews could avoid deportation to the death camps. The 'list' referred to in the film *Schindler's List* was a roll of names he created in 1944 in setting up a branch of the Plaszow concentration camp in his factory compound in Zablocie. Although conditions in the factory were grim, the workers were saved from the gas chamber when Schindler transferred them to a second factory in Brunnlitz, always dodging the Nazis and using his connections and influence to stay one step ahead. He died in 1974 and, at his request, is buried on Mount Zion with his 'children', as he called the Jews he protected.

Opposite: *King David's Tomb is in a building on Mount Zion where the Last Supper is believed by Christians to have taken place.*
Right: *The Dormition Abbey on Mount Zion commemorates the spot where the Virgin Mary is said to have died.*

Mount Zion ★

Mount Zion, a rounded hillock outside the Zion Gate, appears as something rather more substantial in the Bible. It was here that the Virgin Mary is said to have died, a spot now marked by the **Dormition Abbey**. Jesus is also said to have washed the disciples' feet here before the Last Supper.

Symbolic with the promise of a Jewish homeland, Mount Zion has also been the subject of a number of political tussles over the years. Suleiman is supposed to have executed the architect who designed the city walls here for failing to include Mount Zion in what was then Jerusalem.

There is a Catholic cemetery here in which **Oskar Schindler** is buried. Schindler saved the lives of 1200 Jews during the Holocaust and his story was later made into an award-winning movie, *Schindler's List*.

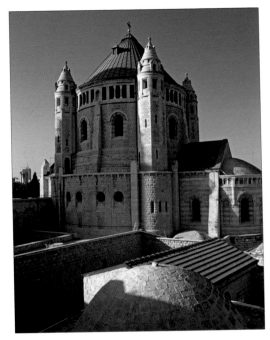

King David's Tomb ★

According to tradition, this building houses David's tomb, as well as the **Room of the Last Supper**, although neither has been proven to be strictly accurate. King David, according to the Bible, is buried on the eastern hill in the City of David, in the opposite direction. In the Byzantine era, however, King David came to be associated with Mount Zion. The Last Supper may have taken place here but the present structure only dates back to the 12th century. The foundations, however, have been dated back to the 2nd century.

The building contains a Romanesque-style hall symbolic of where the Last Supper may have taken place, a synagogue hall, and a Crusader tombstone on top of which is a curtain indicating David's tomb. Climb up the stairs by the minaret to the roof for fine views of the Old City and the Mount of Olives. Open 08:00–17:00 Saturday–Thursday, until 13:00 on Friday.

Mamilla Mall ★

It's a complete change of mood, but if you exit the Old City via the Jaffa Gate, you can pay a visit to the trendy $400-million **Mamilla Mall**, a European-style shopping arcade of chic shops in the subterranean section, the central alleyway open to the skies, and fashionable eating and drinking places on the upper level alongside lavishly expensive condos. From the top, there are stunning views of the city walls and the Tower of David, all floodlit at night, and in summer the Mall is turned into a centre for street entertainment until late. As well as several art galleries and shops selling modern Judaica, you'll find international names like Zara, Nike, Ralph Lauren, Mac and Tommy Hilfiger here. The mall stretches all the way from the Jaffa Gate to **Independence Park**, a large green space a couple of blocks from the main Jaffa Road and a great place for a picnic lunch between museums. The **Mamilla Pool**, part of the park, is part of the water supply system to the Old City.

PARKS IN JERUSALEM

Jerusalem has a number of green spaces, ideal for relaxing after the non-stop round of sightseeing. The parks are maintained by the Jerusalem Foundation, founded in 1966. The largest are Independence Park (Gan Ha-Atzmaut), centrally located in the downtown area of west Jerusalem, and Sacher Park, located near the Knesset and connected with a wooded area known as the Valley of the Cross.

If you're visiting the Knesset, spend some time in the Wohl Rose Garden opposite, containing some 650 varieties of roses. Liberty Bell Park is a popular picnic spot, named after the replica of the US Liberty Bell in Philadelphia that it contains.

Eastern Jerusalem and Around the Walls at a Glance

March to May and late September to October are the best times to visit Jerusalem as the heat is less intense. For detailed tours of the Old City in particular, winter can be a great time as there are hardly any crowds. The weather can be damp and drizzly or, if you're lucky, dazzlingly clear, but take warm clothes either way from November to February. In the middle of summer, visit the Old City and the big attractions around the walls – like the City of David – as early as you can in the morning or late in the evening to avoid both the crowds and the heat. If you are travelling in September, check the dates of Jewish holidays as many attractions will be closed at odd hours during this time.

The closest airport to Jerusalem is Tel Aviv's **Ben Gurion International Airport**, about 40 minutes from the city by **taxi** or *sherut*: Nesher Taxis Sherut, tel: 02 625 7227. There are regular Egged **bus** services from Tel Aviv (www.egged.co.il) and other parts of the country, as well as **trains** from Tel Aviv (www.rail.co.il). You can rent a **car** at Ben Gurion but there is little point if your only destination is Jerusalem, as traffic is bad in the city, not to mention parking. **Public transport** is best for getting to

Jerusalem, and walking is best for getting around.

The areas around East Jerusalem are fairly spread out. You can either plan your day and **walk** most of it and then perhaps take a **taxi** up the Mount of Olives before sunset, or join one of the Egged red double decker **buses** on Route 99, which includes Mount Scopus, the Lion's Gate, the City of David, the Dung Gate and the Jaffa Gate, thus providing a hop-on hop-off service encircling most of the area (except Mount Zion and the Mount of Olives). Don't walk around the Mount of Olives area after dark. If you are in a wheelchair or have trouble walking, visit the excellent website www.accessin israel.org which includes useful information about accessible areas inside the main attractions.

LUXURY
American Colony Hotel, 23 Nablus Road, East Jerusalem, tel: 02 627 9777, www.americancolony.com Romantic and legendary, with colourful history. Popular with visiting diplomats. Gorgeous décor, cocktail bar, pool, three restaurants.
Olive Tree Hotel, 23 St George Street tel: 02 541 0410, www.olivetreehotel.com Large and luxurious

new hotel with architectural touches reflecting the Old City, and an olive tree in the atrium. Restaurant, indoor pool, bar.

MID-RANGE
Grand Court, 15 St George St, tel: 02 591 7777, fax: 02 591 7778, www.grandcourt.com Big hotel with rooftop pool and restaurant; within walking distance of the Damascus Gate.
Mount Zion, 17 Hebron Road, Jerusalem, tel: 02 568 9555, www.mountzion.co.il Landmark hotel in lush gardens near the Old City. Stunning views from the lounge bar.
Jerusalem Hotel, Nablus Road, PO Box 19130, tel: 02 628 3282, fax: 02 628 3282, www.jrshotel.com Beautifully decorated, family-run hotel in old Arab mansion with garden patio designed to simulate a Palestinian village. Popular with media and creative types. Offers tours to Palestinian areas and political tours of Jerusalem.
Jerusalem Pearl, 1 IDF Square, tel: 02 622 6666. Contemporary hotel aimed at observant Jews. Indoor pool, ritual bath, kosher restaurant. Very close to Old City.

BUDGET
Mount of Olives Hotel, 53 Mount of Olives Rd, tel: 02 628 4877, www.mtolives.com Friendly, family-run hotel right next to the Church

of the Ascension with a fun bar under what resembles a Bedouin tent. Stunning views of the Old City.
Golden Walls, Sultan Suleiman St, tel: 02 627 2416, www.goldenwalls. com Budget hotel with restaurant and bar. Near the Damascus Gate.

WHERE TO EAT

Restaurants around East Jerusalem tend to be Arabic in influence, as the area was Jordanian for many years and the Arab traditions continue here. There are also several restaurants strategically positioned around the Old City to enjoy magnificent views over supper.

Lavan, 11 Hebron Road, Cinematheque, tel: 02 673 7393. Classy Italian food overlooking the Old City
Cafe Rimon, Elrov Boulevard, Mamilla, tel: 1 599 501 030. In the swish new Mamilla Mall. Stunning views of the Old City and highly rated dairy and pasta dishes.
Pasha's, 13 Shimon Hazadik Street, tel: 02 582 5162. Palestinian specialities, some exotic (lambs' brains, for example), but plenty of traditional chicken and lamb dishes, great meze and home-made pastries.
Askadinya, 11 Shimon Hazadik Street, tel: 02 532 4590. Creative Italian, French and Palestinian cuisine in a pretty courtyard setting

favoured by the city's opinion-formers.
Blue Dolphin, 7 Shimon Hazadik St, tel: 02 532 2001. Excellent fish restaurant, serving ocean fish and St Peter's fish from Galilee, as well as Lebanese specialities and excellent salads.
Diwan, Jerusalem Hotel (see Where to Stay). Home-cooked Middle Eastern specialities in the fascinating historic setting of a former stable. Have a drink under the vines in the garden first.

SHOPPING

East Jerusalem really isn't the place for shopping, although there is plenty of local colour along the Saladin Street and a lively produce market around the Damascus Gate, frequented by locals as well as tourists. The **Mamilla Mall**, just outside Jaffa Gate, is a huge attraction and full of designer goods and smart cafés but most of the main shopping areas are slightly further west, along Jaffa Road and beyond.

TOURS AND EXCURSIONS

Apart from the Route 99 bus (see Getting Around), most of the standard city tours include the sights around the Walls, the Mount of Olives and Mount Zion. Guided tours are offered by numerous operators. Try **Jerusalem Experience**, tel: 077 558 6001, www.jerusalem experience.co.il for small

group tours (up to six) with different themes – Jewish, Three Religions, King David, for example. **Alternative Tours** (tel: 0522 864 205, www.alternativetours.ps) offers political tours of the Old City and East Jerusalem, with an emphasis on inter-acting with local people and putting forward the Palestinian viewpoint while showing you the sights.
Green Olive Tours (tel: 03 721 9540, www.toursin english.com) also offers tours with a political theme, even taking visitors to meet Jewish settlers on the occupied West Bank. The idea is to expand the political debate beyond 'Us and Them'.
Alternatively you can book a **private tour guide**; all guides registered with the tourist board are listed, with the languages they speak, on www.goisrael.com
For something different, take a **Segway Tour** of the City of David, 90 minutes around Jerusalem's oldest neighbour-hood on personal electric two-wheeled vehicles. Tours leave from the Peace Forest daily at 10:30; tel: 02 626 2341, www.cityofdavid.org.il

USEFUL CONTACTS

Tourist Information Centre Ministry of Tourism, Jaffa Gate, tel: 02 627 1422.
Local information:
www.jerusalemite.net
Police, 1 Saladin St, tel: 02 626 1378.

7
West Jerusalem

Jerusalem's development has spread far beyond the tangled lanes and solid ramparts of the original Old City into relatively new neighbourhoods such as the wonderfully atmospheric **German Colony** and **Yemin Moshe**. Hopeful immigrants arrived in Jerusalem in the 19th century to start a new life, building themselves smart little enclaves with views of the Old City, and today these represent some of the city's most desirable residential areas.

Meanwhile, along the main thoroughfare of **Jaffa Road**, 21st-century Jerusalem is very much in evidence as restaurants, cafés, shops and nightclubs jostle for space around the **Ben Yehuda Pedestrian Mall** and in the tight-knit lanes of the 19th-century **Nahalat Shiva**. Around Agripas Street you'll find the colourful and vibrant **Mahane Yehuda Market** and any number of small museums and galleries.

Many important monuments and museums are located in the western areas of Jerusalem, where architects have had the space to stretch their imagination and express themselves with breathtaking, contemporary designs. Just west of the main shopping area is the huge **Sacher Park**, a green expanse housing the **Supreme Court** and the **Knesset** parliament building, as well as the stunning **Shrine of the Book** at the **Israel Museum**. To the southwest, there's more green space at the **Biblical Zoo**, a great day out for children, while on the western city limits, gazing out over peaceful pine forests and the cypress groves of **Mount Herzl**, is

DON'T MISS

★★★ **Yad Vashem:** the most moving memorial imaginable.
★★★ **Shrine of the Book:** see the Dead Sea Scrolls.
★★ Enjoy a night out in the **German Colony** with its fantastic restaurants.
★★ **The Biblical Zoo:** perfect for families.
★★ **Ein Kerem village:** best on a Saturday at lunchtime.

Opposite: The ceiling of the Shrine of the Book is designed to resemble one of the jars in which the Dead Sea Scrolls were housed.

HIKES NEAR JERUSALEM

Jerusalem is surrounded by woods and forests. The **Jerusalem Forest** to the west has been planted with some six million trees in memory of the Jewish victims of the Holocaust. In the same direction is **Nahal Sorek**, located beyond the rich suburb of Ein Kerem and containing some caves with stalactite and stalagmite formations.

Wadi Qelt, between Jerusalem and Jericho, is a desert gorge with a nature reserve, spring, waterfall and aqueduct. It is also the site of the picturesque St George's Monastery, cut into the side of a cliff. Wadi Qelt and Nahal Sorek are popular hiking spots, although Wadi Qelt has been the site of a number of Palestinian attacks on tourists, including six murders in the 1990s. If you want to hike in these areas, make sure you are aware of the security situation and that travel here is not advised against.

The **Dead Sea** and its surrounds are also an easy drive and a major location for outdoor activities.

possibly the most important museum of all, the Holocaust memorial of **Yad Vashem**.

Time Elevator ★★

The Time Elevator at 37 Hillel Street is a great cheat's guide to the history of Jerusalem. It's a white-knuckle ride, ideal if you have children or if you're a big kid yourself, or if you just need a crash course in history! **Chaim Topol**, famous star of the film *Fiddler on the Roof*, narrates 3000 years of drama, from the City of David to the 1967 Six Day War via the destruction of the First and Second Temples, the birth of Christianity and the emergence of Islam. Moving seats, surround sound and special effects guarantee you'll feel part of history itself. Open Monday–Thursday 10:00–17:00, Friday 10:00–14:00 and Saturday 12:00–18:00. Over fives only; stationary seats are provided for those who prefer, such as pregnant women. Get there 15 minutes early for a safety briefing.

Artists' House ★

Located in the former art academy, established in the early 20th century by **Boris Schatz**, the Artists' House comprises three floors of exhibition halls showcasing the work of Israeli and international artists. The building also accommodates the **Bezalel Academy for Arts and Design**; previously, it was the Bezalel National Museum, predecessor to the huge Israel Museum. The Artists' House aims to promote the work of young as well as established artists and has constantly changing exhibitions. It's worth a visit – you may even spot the next big thing! It is open Sunday–Thursday 10:00–13:00 and 16:00–19:00; Friday 10:00–13:00; Saturday 11:00–14:00.

Mahane Yehuda ★★★

Mahane Yehuda is Jerusalem's answer to Tel Aviv's famous Carmel Market: a huge, bustling **food market** selling everything from chocolate-flavoured halva to mysterious medicinal potions. Locals come here to do

Left: *Mahane Yehuda Market sells everything, from food to clothing.*

their weekly shop and tourists come to assemble a picnic for the day – you can even buy corkscrews and wine glasses, as well as fine **Israeli wines**. There are great piles of delicious fresh fruit, the aromas of freshly baked bread wafting from the bakeries, stalls with every imaginable type of cheese (Israelis are great cheese eaters) as well as specialist herb and even natural medicine vendors. There are fashion stalls, too, mainly selling knock-off designer labels. The hubbub reaches fever pitch on Friday afternoons as locals prepare for the Sabbath. Open Sunday–Thursday 09:00–20:00; Friday 09:00 until one hour before Sabbath (dusk).

Museum on the Seam ★

A short walk from the Old City, before you get to Me'a She'arim, pay a call at the Museum on the Seam, a unique, **socio-political contemporary art museum** dedicated to liberty, respect, human rights, listening and discussion about different ideologies. The exhibitions change constantly but all provoke thought and debate. It is open Sunday–Thursday 09:00–17:00 and Friday 09:00–14:00.

ISRAELI WINE

Return visitors to Israel will notice that the local wine has vastly improved over the past decade, due to refinements in growing and winemaking technique. Some of the Cabernet Sauvignons or Bordeaux-style blends are excellent. Malbec is relatively new and Petit Verdot is being used in some prestigious blends.

Israel also makes sparkling wines, dessert wines and Chardonnays, as well as Sauvignon Blancs, Gewürztraminers and White Rieslings, some of the best whites coming from the Golan Heights. Total annual production is reckoned to be 35 million bottles.

THE ULTRA-ORTHODOX

The ultra-Orthodox Jews, known as Haredim, practise what they believe is the purest form of Judaism and live in closed communities, avoiding contact with the outside world where possible. Prayer, study of the Torah and family are the most important aspects of life, and modern trappings like TV and the Internet are frowned upon. Their move-ment has its own economy, medical services, welfare system and education system and, in Israel, they do not serve in the army. Dress code varies among Hassidic and non-Hassidic Haredim, but takes its inspiration from how the 18th- and 19th-century East European Jews dressed, in dark suits. Wide-brimmed hats are worn and men have long beards and side-locks. Women dress modestly and cover their heads with hats, scarves or wigs.

Me'a She'arim ★★

A few blocks north of Zion Square is the fascinating ultra-Orthodox Jewish neighbourhood, reminiscent of a pre-war East European *shtetl*, of Me'a She'arim, built in 1875 as a refuge for the ultra-Orthodox Hassidim. Walking through the narrow streets is like stepping back in time, the alleys lined with old synagogues and grey buildings. The devout residents, many pale-faced and bespectacled, sport black hats, long black robes and long, curly side-locks of hair. Women are extremely modestly dressed and do not reveal uncovered heads; they either wear wigs or hats. The ultra-Orthodox men spend most of their time studying the **Talmud**, although some run businesses. Visitors are welcome but respect-ful dress and behaviour must be taken very seriously. Do not visit on a Friday afternoon or Saturday, when the Sabbath is observed.

Yemin Moshe ★★

One of the most desirable addresses in Jerusalem today is Yemin Moshe, overlooking the Old City and topped by a **stone windmill**. Its pretty stone buildings were the homes of the first Jewish colony to settle outside the safety of the city walls, in the 1860s.

The patron of the colony, the English-Jewish phil-anthropist **Sir Moses Montefiore**, visited Jerusalem in

1858 and was so appalled by the cramped conditions within the walls of the city that he decided to sponsor a new suburb. He enlisted wealthy New Orleans Jew, **Judah Touro**, to help with the ambitious project.

Notable features apart from the windmill are the **Mishkenot Sha'ananim**, a long, single-storey building on Yemin Moshe Street which has been restored as a guesthouse for visiting artists and authors who have been invited to Jerusalem by the authorities in order to take inspiration from the atmosphere and beautiful

Opposite: *Life in Me'a She'arim is virtually unchanged since the days of the East European ghettoes.*

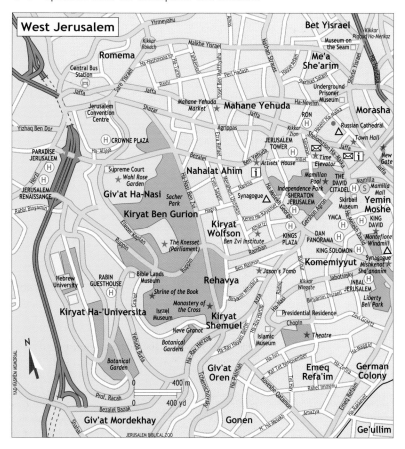

West Jerusalem

Yirmeyahu · Kikkar Piqqud Ha-Merkaz · Bet Yisrael · Museum on the Seam · Me'a She'arim · Kikkar Rokach · Malkhe Yisrael · Nathan Strauss · Shivte Yisrael · Romema · Ha-Hashmona'im · Ha-Turim · Tsefaniah · Yosef Ben Matityahu · Peri Hadash · Shmuel Salant · Central Bus Station · Rashi · Jaffa · Jaffa · Shazar · Mahane Yehuda Market · Mahane Yehuda · Jaffa · Ha-Nevi'im · Underground Prisoner Museum · Morasha · Jerusalem Convention Centre · Agrippas · Ezra Refael · RON · Russian Cathedral · Yizhaq Ben Dor · CROWNE PLAZA · Kikkar Zion · JERUSALEM TOWER · Shelomziyon Ha-Malka · Town Hall · PARADISE JERUSALEM · Ha-Aliyya · Bezalel · Ben Yehuda · Artists' House · Hillel · Jaffa · New Gate · Time Elevator · JERUSALEM RENAISSANCE · Supreme Court · Wohl Rose Garden · Nahalat Ahim · Mamillan Pool · THE DAVID CITADEL · Mamilla · Mamilla Mall · Rabbi Binyamin · Giv'at Ha-Nasi · Sacher Park · Menahem Ussishkin · Independence Park · SHERATON JERUSALEM · Gershon Agron · Skirball Museum · Yemin Moshe · Kiryat Ben Gurion · Hagra · Keren Ha-Kayemet · Gershon George · YMCA · KING DAVID · Eliezer Kaplan · Kiryat Wolfson · Aharizi · KINGS PLAZA · DAN PANORAMA · Ha-Melekh David · Montefiore Windmill · Ruppin · The Knesset (Parliament) · Ben Zvi Institute · Ramban · KING SOLOMON · Komemiyyut · Mishkenot Sha'ananim · Synagogue · Ben Maimon · Jason's Tomb · Rehavya · Kikkar Wingate · Jabotinsky · INBAL JERUSALEM · Hebrew University · RABIN GUESTHOUSE · Bible Lands Museum · Ruppin · Binyamin Mtudela · Ha-Nasi · Binyamin Disraeli · Liberty Bell Park · Kiryat Ha-'Universita · Granot · Shrine of the Book · Monastery of the Cross · Israel Museum · Kiryat Shemuel · Binyamin · Ha-Rav Berlin · Chopin · Presidential Residence · Tsvi Graetz · Neve Granot · Ha-Rav Hayyim Berlin · Islamic Museum · Theatre · Yehuda Burla · Botanical Gardens · Ha-Rav Herzog · Giv'at Oren · Ha-Ivri · Emeq Refa'im · German Colony · Botanical Garden · Ha-Palmah · Kaf Tet beNovember · Koveshe Qatamon · Ha-Lleh · Rahel Immenu · Ha-Zefira · Ha-Maggid · Prof. Racah · Chernichovsky · Gonen · H. Ha-Melakh · Amazya · Emeq Refa'im · Ha-Rakkevet · Giv'at Mordekhay · Bezalel Bazak · JERUSALEM BIBLICAL ZOO · Ge'ullim

0 · 400 m · 0 · 400 yd

N

YAD VASHEM MEMORIAL

views up here. Further along the street is the **Sephardic Synagogue**, in an area dating back to the 1890s once inhabited by immigrants from Turkey, who arrived in 1948. These immigrants were relocated when the government decided to turn Yemin Moshe into an artists' colony but their descendants continue to attend the synagogue today.

Yemin Moshe was badly damaged in the 1967 war but was rebuilt and soon established itself as a fashionable, artistic neighbourhood. The windmill at the top was a working structure, providing flour for the colony, although it was something of a pipe dream as the equipment brought from England failed to work properly in Jerusalem and there wasn't enough wind at the site. In 1948, it served as an important observation post for the Israeli army. Now it's a small museum depicting the life of **Montefiore**. It is open 09:00–16:00 Sunday–Thursday; 09:00–13:00 Friday.

King David Hotel ★

Located on Ha-Melekh David Street, this hotel is a Jerusalem landmark, constructed out of the local honey-coloured stone and opened in 1931. Kings, queens and heads of state have visited or even lived here, among them Emperor **Haile Selassie of Ethiopia**, who was driven out by the Italians in 1936, and **King George II of**

Right: *The King David Hotel is a city landmark and the chosen residence of visiting dignitaries and celebrities.*

Greece, who set up his government in exile at the hotel after the Nazi occupation of his country in 1942.

The British used the building as a base during the Mandate Period and a whole wing was blown up in July 1946 by the Jewish underground group **Irgun**, who hid bombs in milk churns. Bomb warnings were ignored and 91 people died, with 45 injured, leading to calls for the British to withdraw from Israel. When they eventually did, in 1948, the hotel, by now a Jewish stronghold, found itself overlooking the **Armistice Line** between Israeli and Jordanian territory.

The hotel was bought by Israel's leading hotel group, Dan Hotels, in 1958 and remains the city's most prestigious accommodation to this day, having hosted famous names, from Bill Clinton to Tony Blair and Madonna.

YMCA ★

Opposite the King David Hotel, the YMCA is another celebrated building and certainly one of the most spectacular YMCAs in the world. It was designed in 1928–33 by architects Shreve, Lamb and Harmon, who were also responsible for the Empire State Building in New York City. Not unlike the graceful minaret of a mosque, the 35m (120ft) tower offers stunning views of the city, and throughout the building there is symbolism of the three monotheistic faiths, underlining the YMCA's mission, to foster inter-faith, inter-racial and inter-group understanding. The building is actually a four-star hotel now, rather than the more humble and typical YMCA, but still works to its original principles and was nominated for a **Nobel Peace Prize** in 1993 for its efforts in promoting peace and unity.

German Colony ★★

The German Colony is one of the city's most desirable residential areas, its broad streets lined with shady pine and eucalyptus trees, with clusters of fashionable cafés and restaurants. The colony was built by **German Templar Knights** over 100 years ago and the elegant

---

JERUSALEM FOR CHILDREN

Many of Jerusalem's attractions are relevant to children. Start on your way there at **Mini Israel**, a popular family attraction. Children will love the interactive displays at the **Tower of David Museum** and the **Ramparts Walk**. **Zedekiah's Cave** is fun for families and equally interesting, if a little more 'serious', are the **Western Wall Tunnels**. Teenagers will enjoy the Segway tours of the **City of David**. The **Israel Museum** has a Youth Wing ideal for all ages. For fresh air, the **Jerusalem Biblical Zoo** is both educational and fun, and you can get there on the open-top tour bus, another bonus.

TORAH OR TALMUD?

You'll hear in Jewish circles reference to the Torah and the Talmud. There is a difference. The written Torah is the five books of Moses given to the Jews by God at Mount Sinai; it is open to interpretation and is the subject of great debate. The Talmud is the oral Torah which, while it was handed down verbally through generations for centuries, is a series of volumes concerning the application of Jewish religious law in everyday life.

JOSEPH, INTERPRETER OF DREAMS

Favourite son of Jacob, Joseph was envied by his 11 brothers, who sold him as a slave to a pharaoh. Joseph, however, could interpret dreams and won the favour of the pharaoh by prophesying seven years of feast followed by seven years of famine. The pharaoh made Joseph his highest official and charged him with collecting food to be used during the years of famine. When the famine arrived, the Egyptians were able to survive as a result. The brothers came to Egypt, begging for food, and the family was reconciled.

Below: *Contemporary sculpture, Israel Museum.*

mansions and tree-lined streets could be an affluent suburb of a modern German city.

The German Colony is a good place to come for an evening, or for late-afternoon people-watching in the sunny street cafés like **Caffit**, a Jerusalem institution. There are several theatres here, too, including the art-house **Cinematheque** cinema, the **Khan Theatre**, build around an old Bedouin caravanserai, and **The Lab**, a hip bar with live music and temporary art exhibitions.

Israel Museum and the Shrine of the Book ★★★

The spectacular Israel Museum is an essential stop on a tour of Jerusalem. The museum covers art, archaeology, ethnology and its highlight is the **Dead Sea Scrolls**. It is under renovation at the time of writing, with several brand new areas opening in 2010. You can't miss it from a distance, as the Shrine of the Book is a curious peaked dome shape, resembling the lids of the stone caskets in which the original scrolls were stored.

Start with the amazing **scale model of Jerusalem** in the Second Temple Period, from 516BC. A guide is very helpful here, although you can rent audio guides from the visitor centre. Next, there's a slightly odd film about the mysterious sect who lived at **Qumran**, the barren place near the Dead Sea where the scrolls were found. It's more about the life of the unfeasibly scrubbed and good-looking group of young men that lived there than the scrolls themselves, but is worth a look nonetheless.

The highlight, however, is the Shrine of the Book, at the centre of which is displayed the **Book of Isaiah**, the oldest biblical document known to man. The scrolls themselves, fragile scraps of parchment beautifully laid out under glass, are awe-inspiring. Many others, of course, are safely stored in archives.

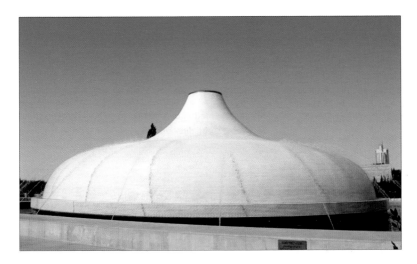

To understand more about the times of the **Old Testament**, you can visit the breathtaking archaeological section where 6000-year-old pottery figures, Caananite sarcophagi and 4000-year-old metalwork are housed, alongside tomb inscriptions dating from the time of Jesus.

The art areas include sections of Jewish art, and some good Impressionist work including Renoirs and Van Goghs. Outside, stroll through the attractive **Billy Rose Sculpture Gardens**. Wild herbs grow amongst the orderly flower beds and sculptures and there are magnificent views of the city. Open 10:00–17:00 Sunday, Monday, Wednesday, Thursday and Saturday; 16:00–21:00 Tuesday; and 10:00–14:00 Friday.

Bible Lands Museum ★

If you're especially keen on biblical history, drop into the nearby Bible Lands Museum to see a remarkable collection of coins, pottery, weapons and frescoes from the regions featured in the Bible. There are permanent and temporary exhibitions displaying artefacts from **Rome** and **ancient Greece**, and cultural evenings on Saturday nights with wine and cheese and live music.

Above: *The Shrine of the Book is one of Israel's top visitor attractions.*

DEAD SEA SCROLLS

The discovery of the Dead Sea Scrolls between 1947 and 1956 was one of the most important finds in history. The scrolls were discovered in 11 caves along the northwest shore of the Dead Sea, near Qumran, known to be the home of the Essene sect in biblical times. There were between 825 and 870 scrolls in tens of thousands of fragments, made of animal skins and papyrus and written in a carbon-based ink. The virtually intact Isaiah Scroll is 1000 years older than any previously known copy of Isaiah and is on display in the Shrine of the Book today.

The Knesset ★

Israel's fortress-like parliament building was completed in 1966, designed by **Josef Klarvin** and financed by **Baron James de Rothschild**. You can visit by prior arrangement; to find out when there are guided tours in English, tel: 02 675 3416. The parliamentary sessions are open to the public on Mondays and Tuesdays at 16:00 and Wednesdays at 11:00. These are, of course, in Hebrew only.

The Supreme Court ★

A short walk from the Knesset is the Supreme Court, also open to the public, with free guided tours in English Sunday–Thursday at 12:00. Although the building was only completed in 1992, it's packed with symbolism of Judaism and justice, different architectural elements of the building inspired by sayings from the Old Testament. Do take the tour, or some of the most fascinating aspects may pass you by.

Wohl Rose Garden ★

The Supreme Court and the Knesset are connected via a beautiful rose garden, in bloom almost year-round thanks to the huge abundance of roses of different types planted here. It's a short but very pleasant walk around the gardens and there's a small lake, too – a good spot for a picnic.

Yad Vashem Memorial ★★★

Yad Vashem, the museum and memorial dedicated to the six million victims of the **Holocaust**, is probably the most important monument you will see in Jerusalem and indeed, in the whole of Israel. Situated on **Mount Herzl** in the city's far west, it is brilliantly designed, deeply moving, extremely depressing and uplifting at the same time. So powerful are the images that children under the age of 10 are not allowed in. Give yourself plenty of time to visit – at least two hours, probably half a day – and allow time for contemplation afterwards as you will probably not feel like rushing off and doing something else.

The main exhibit, the **Holocaust History Museum**, is a masterful piece of design in the shape of a triangular prism. You enter at one end and emerge at the other – there is no way out in between. The prism descends below ground level, emerging again symbolically into the light, the long glass strip in the ceiling illuminating the darkness below at its deepest point.

Off the prism are different rooms with exhibitions telling the story from the point of view of the victims, a mixture of harrowing film of the ghettoes, awful statistics, artefacts, personal testimonies, memorabilia and multimedia montages. At one point, there's a cutaway cattle train carriage.

The prism emerges back into sunlight at the end, with an uninterrupted view across forested hills. But this is only a fraction of Yad Vashem. Visit the **Hall of Names**, a dome-shaped structure with hundreds of thousands of images of people who were murdered by the Nazis gazing down from the ceiling. The top of the dome is open to the elements and below is a dark pool, reflecting the faces above, a symbol that they won't be forgotten. Of the six million Jews killed, only three million have

Below: *The grounds of the moving Yad Vashem Memorial house many important pieces of sculpture.*

Above: *Thousands of faces gaze down from the ceiling in the Hall of Names.*

THE LAW OF RETURN

More Jews live away from Israel than in it, following waves of Diaspora over the centuries, but Israel states a right to return for all Jews who express a desire to live in the country, in a law passed in 1950. Returning to live in Israel is known as *aliyah*, which literally means 'ascent', and Jews say they 'make *aliyah*'. A person making *aliyah* is an *oleh*, plural *olim*. *Olim* have the right to settle and work in Israel. The law applies to anyone with at least one grandparent who was born Jewish and those who have converted to Judaism.

been accounted for. There is a massive archive at Yad Vashem, the world's largest, with both paper and electronic records, and visitors are welcome to sit and document the details of their own lost relatives.

Another profoundly moving (and difficult) monument is the **Children's Memorial**, a tribute to the 1.5 million children who died at the hands of the Nazis. The memorial is underground and dark inside, lit only by candles. Visitors feel their way by means of a handrail, while pictures of children appear above out of the darkness, a voice intoning their name, age and country of origin.

There are many other areas for quiet contemplation. In the **Hall of Remembrance**, a basalt structure with the names of 22 of the hundreds of murder sites engraved on the floor, a flame burns continuously next to a crypt containing the ashes of victims retrieved from the concentration camps. The **Valley of the Communities** is an amazing piece of sculpture, a 1ha (2.5-acre) monument carved out of the bedrock. You'll see the names of 5000 Jewish communities that were either totally or almost totally eradicated carved onto 107 walls.

Somewhat more uplifting is the **Avenue of the Righteous Among the Nations**, a path lined with trees planted in honour of the non-Jews who risked their own lives during the Holocaust. A plaque is dedicated to each person, the gestures of whom leave you with some faith in human nature after a visit to this tragic place. Open Sunday–Thursday 09:00–17:00 and Friday 09:00–14:00 (www.yadvashem.org).

Herzl Museum ★

On the same hill is the museum dedicated to **Theodor Herzl**, the Viennese lawyer and writer credited with the foundation of Zionism. The museum details his life and the contributions he made to the Zionist cause. His black granite tomb can be seen on the hilltop outside. The museum is open 08:30–16:30 Sunday–Thursday; 08:30–13:30 Friday.

Ein Kerem ★★

One of the prettiest neighbourhoods is Ein Kerem, a popular place to visit for lunch on Saturdays. Lots of wealthy diplomats live here, in beautiful houses

> **MOSHE SAFDIE**
>
> Moshe Safdie, the Haifa-born architect of Yad Vashem, has won multiple awards for his work, known worldwide for its geometric patterns, use of light and incorporation of open space. His work in Israel includes the Mamilla Mall in Jerusalem, the graves of Yitzhak and Leah Rabin, and the dramatic Terminal 3 building at Ben Gurion Airport. Outside Israel, notable projects include the United States Institute of Peace in Washington DC, the Kaufmann Center for the Performing Arts in Kansas City, and the Centre in Vancouver for the Performing Arts. He was also part of the team that refurbished Old Jerusalem after the city was reunified in 1967.

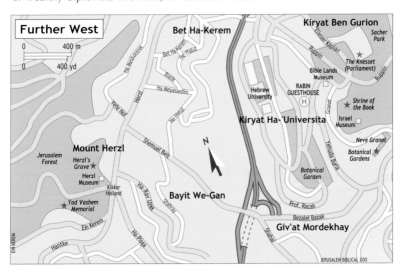

Above: *Israelis love to while away the time at Jerusalem's many street cafés.*

with amazing views of the surrounding Judean Hills, which are cloaked in wild pomegranate, olive, fig and pear trees overlooked by ranks of tall, graceful cypresses.

Ein Kerem has a number of historical significances, hence the large number of churches here. Christians believe it to be the birthplace of **John the Baptist** and also the place where the Virgin Mary visited **Elizabeth**, the mother of John, when she (Mary) was pregnant with Jesus. There is indeed a natural spring here, which emerges at various spots in the village and was probably the origin of the settlement here.

Notable buildings include the convent and guesthouse of **Notre Dame de Sion**, built in the hills overlooking the village, and the **Church of St John the Baptist**, which houses the grotto where St John the Baptist is believed to have been born. The church was originally a **Byzantine sanctuary** and was rebuilt in 1674. Today it is rich with Spanish paintings and medieval art. Open 08:00–12:00 and 14:30–18:00 daily except Sundays, when the church closes at 17:00.

In the compact centre you'll find some excellent restaurants for lunch, which get very crowded on Saturdays. If you're looking for home-made chocolate and Italian ice cream, or Lebanese specialities, or a huge brunch in the sunshine, this is the place to come.

Jerusalem Biblical Zoo ★

A 25ha (62-acre) site around a lake to the southwest of Jerusalem is home to the animals of the much-loved Jerusalem Biblical Zoo, which has had several incarnations around the city. This non-profit animal park is dedicated to **conservation** and **captive breeding** and has a special emphasis on animals mentioned in the Bible, although if you start to count through the species discussed in the Bible, it's an almost endless list, from frogs and locusts to donkeys and camels! There are plenty of

---

THE SHEPHERD'S FIELDS

A visit to Bethlehem would not be complete without seeing the fields where shepherds watched their flocks and saw the angles proclaiming the birth of Christ. Go by taxi or walk the short distance along the imaginatively named Shepherd's Street off Manger Square to the Arab village of Beit Salur. Two churches mark the spot where the shepherds were supposedly sitting: a Greek church stands in the field, while the Franciscan Church of the Angels covers the caves where the shepherds lived.

animals to see, including two spectacular Sumatran tigers, Syrian brown bears, Persian leopards and biblical creatures such as oryx, ibex and gazelle. There's an information centre and auditorium in a wooden **Noah's Ark** (Noah being the original conservationist), a children's zoo, a zoo train, a snack bar and coffee shop. Open Sunday–Thursday 09:00–18:00; Friday 09:00–16:30; Saturday 10:00–18:00. Get there on the No. 99 Tourist Bus or the No. 26 from the central bus station.

Mini Israel ★

This hugely popular family attraction is ideal as a stop on the drive between Tel Aviv and Jerusalem, displaying 350 **scale models** of Israel's most famous sights, on a scale of 1:25. You'll see the airport, the beaches of Tel Aviv, Old Jaffa, the Al-Aqsa Mosque and the Dome of the Rock in Jerusalem, the Yemin Moshe windmill, the Old City, Masada, the coral reef observatory in Eilat … although the layout isn't true to Israel's long, narrow shape, you should leave with a pretty good idea of the country's main attractions and children will love the working models of trains, planes and marching soldiers. Open Sunday–Thursday and Saturday 10:00–18:00, and Friday 10:00–14:00.

KING DAVID'S WELL

Also in Bethlehem is David's Well, consisting of three rock-hewn water cisterns, situated on Manger Street opposite the King David Cinema. During a battle with the Philistines, King David sent three of his men to break through the Philistine ranks to fetch water. But when they returned, the king sacrificed the water to God, rather than 'drink the blood of the men who went at the risk of their lives'.

Below: *Mini Israel presents a potted history of the country in a series of remarkable scale models.*

West Jerusalem at a Glance

BEST TIMES TO VISIT

March to May and late September to October are the best times to visit Jerusalem as the heat is less intense. For detailed tours of the Old City in particular, winter can be a great time as there are hardly any crowds. The weather can be damp and drizzly or, if you're lucky, dazzlingly clear, but take warm clothes either way from November to February. In the middle of summer, visit the big outdoor attractions as early as you can in the morning or late in the evening to avoid both the crowds and the heat. If you are travelling in September, check the dates of Jewish holidays as many attractions will be closed at odd hours during this time. The best time to visit the suburb of Ein Kerem is Saturday lunchtime.

GETTING THERE

The closest airport to Jerusalem is Tel Aviv's **Ben Gurion International Airport**, about 40 minutes from the city by **taxi** or *sherut*: Nesher Taxis Sherut, tel: 02 625 7227. There are regular Egged **bus** services from Tel Aviv (www.egged.co.il) and other parts of the country, as well as **trains** from Tel Aviv (www.rail.co.il). You can rent a **car** at Ben Gurion but there is little point if your only destination is Jerusalem, as traffic is bad in the city, not to mention parking.
Taxis: HaPalmach, tel: 02

679 3333; HaUma, tel: 02 538 9999; Smadar, tel: 02 566 4444.
Car Rental: Budget, 23 King David St, tel: 02 624 8991; Eldan, 24 King David St, tel: 02 625 2151; Hertz, 19 King David St, tel: 02 581 5069.

GETTING AROUND

Jaffa Road and Yemin Moshe are walkable but you will need transport to venture further afield to Mount Herzl or the Knesset area, or the Biblical Zoo. Join one of the Egged red double decker **buses** on Route 99, which includes all of these and provides a hop-on hop-off service encircling the whole of the west of the city. Alternatively, there are regular buses all over the city – use the interactive route planner on www.egged.co.il If you are in a wheelchair or have trouble walking, visit the excellent website www.accessinisrael.org which includes useful information about accessible areas inside the main attractions.

WHERE TO STAY

West Jerusalem is where all the big luxury hotels are located, so there is plenty of choice.

LUXURY
The King David Hotel, 23 King David Street, tel: 02 620 8888, www.kingdavidhotel.co.il Luxurious flagship of the Dan Hotels chain, favoured by

VIPs and offering beautiful views of the Old City.
The David Citadel Hotel, 7 King David Street, tel: 02 621 1111, www.thedavidcitadel.com Luxury five-star hotel facing the Old City. Family-friendly, with heated pool.
Inbal Jerusalem Hotel, 3 Jabotinsky Street, tel: 02 675 6666, www.inbalhotel.com Five-star resort hotel built in Jerusalem stone near Yemin Moshe with views of the Old City and Liberty Bell Park.

MID-RANGE
Dan Boutique Hotel, 31 Hebron Rd, tel: 03 520 2552, fax: 03 548 0111, www.dan hotels.com Petite version of the bigger Dan Hotels, with rooftop gym, chic bar, amazing views of the Old City and Mount Zion and within walking distance of Yemin Moshe and the German Colony.
The Three Arches Hotel, at the Jerusalem YMCA, 26 King David Street, tel: 02 569 2692, www.ymca3arch.co.il One of the world's most famous YMCAs, now operating as a four-star hotel but keeping the principles of tolerance and inclusion associated with YMCA.

BUDGET
St Andrew's Scottish Guesthouse, 1 David Remez Street, tel: 02 673 2401, www.scotsguesthouse.com A little slice of Scottish hos-

West Jerusalem at a Glance

pitality in the centre of Jerusalem; comfortable 19-room guesthouse attached to the St Andrews Scottish Church.
Rabin Guesthouse, Nahman Avigad 1, Giv'at Ram, tel: 02 678 0101, fax: 02 679 6566, www.iyha.org.il A 77-room guesthouse/youth hostel built in local stone in memory of Yitzhak Rabin. Rooms with private facilities. Restaurant.
Jerusalem Hostel, 44 Jaffa Road, tel: 02 623 6102, fax: 02 623 6092. Right on Zion Square, handy for all the nightlife. Rooms with bathroom; roof terrace.

WHERE TO EAT

Tamago Sushi, 48 Emek Refaim Street, tel: 077 515 0140. Kosher and highly rated Japanese food served in a restored Templar mansion in the German Colony.
La Boca, 46 Emek Refaim Street, tel: 02 563 5577, http://laboca.rest-e.co.il Real Latin-American food (kosher) served in a second-floor restaurant in a gorgeous old mansion in the German Colony. Fantastic steaks and South American wines.
Caffit, 35 Emek Refaim St, tel: 02 563 5284. Fashionable café with indoor and outdoor seating; busy all day. Kosher dairy with fantastic salads, soups and pasta.
Luchana, 27 Emek Refaim St, tel: 02 563 0111. Trendy Italian dairy/fish restaurant in the German Colony, with a beautiful terrace.

Hafinjan, 82 Agrippas St, tel: 02 622 2241. Good, basic Israeli food (hummus, falafel and stews) served near the market at Mahane Yehuda.
Dagim BeHazer, 31 Jaffa St, Feingold Yard, tel: 02 622 2524. Welcoming fish restaurant in the heart of the nightlife area of Jaffa Street. Great food, friendly service.
Olive and Fish, 2 Jabotinsky St, tel: 02 566 5020, www.2eat.co.il/eng/oliveandfish/ High-class kosher fish and meat restaurant near Yemin Moshe; creative cooking and romantic atmosphere.
Montefiore, Under the Windmill, Yemin Moshe, tel: 02 623 2928, www.2eat.co.il/eng/montefiore/ Kosher dairy with wonderful cheesy pastas, salads and decadent desserts.

SHOPPING

Jaffa Road is the city's main shopping area, lined with clothes and accessories shops spilling over into the narrow alleys off the main thoroughfare and the Ben Yehuda Pedestrian Mall. Don't miss the market at Mahane Yehuda for food, wine, household goods and souvenirs. At one end of Jaffa Road is the new Mamilla Mall, a great place to shop for designer goods, a stone's throw from the Jaffa Gate of the Old City.

TOURS AND EXCURSIONS

Most of the big museums do guided tours in English, including Yad Vashem and

the Israel Museum, as well as the Knesset and the Supreme Court. You can also rent an audio-guide in Yad Vashem. The Egged Bus No. 99 stops at all the big attractions and offers commentary in eight languages, although it doesn't include entrance fees. If you can stretch to a **private guide**, it's a good idea, as some of the museums are big and complex; there's a list on www.goisrael.com
The **Municipality of Jerusalem** offers free walking tours with qualified guides. Meet by the palm trees on Safra Square at 10:00 daily; tel: 02 531 4600 for times and dates, as there's a huge variety of tours. For guided tours, try **Jerusalem Experience**, tel: 077 558 6001, www.jerusalem experience.co.il for small group tours (up to six) with different themes – Jewish, Three Religions, King David, for example. Or book a **private tour guide**, tel: 03 751 1132, or visit http://itga.org.il/english

USEFUL CONTACTS

Tourist Information Centre Ministry of Tourism, Jaffa Gate, tel: 02 627 1422.
Local information: www.tour. jerusalem.muni.il/eng/ or visit the informative local blog www.jerusalemite.net
National tourist board: www.goisrael.com
Police: 1 Saladin Street, tel: 02 626 1378.

8
Excursions from Tel Aviv and Jerusalem

The reality of travel in Israel is that the country is so small, you can get almost anywhere in a day and it is certainly worth exploring beyond the city limits of Tel Aviv and Jerusalem, entrancing though they are.

Tel Aviv is just one of a string of fascinating settlements on Israel's fertile coastal plain. Heading northwards along the coast you will find **Roman Caesarea**, the cosmopolitan city of **Haifa**, home to the Baha'i faith, and **Akko**, with its magnificent underground Crusader city, before the landscape buckles up into the sometimes snow-covered mountains of the Golan Heights. Inland from the coast is the beautiful, tranquil **Sea of Galilee** and a number of important Christian sites, including Nazareth.

Jerusalem, meanwhile, itself less than an hour from Tel Aviv, is the gateway to the **Dead Sea**, the **Judean Hills** and the desert beyond. This is one of Israel's most 'biblical' landscapes: low, rolling hills dotted with dusty olive trees, grazing donkeys and goats, rocky terraces, Bedouin encampments, and grubby children playing in the dust. From the hills outside Jerusalem it is easy to spot the distant blue, metallic glint of the **Dead Sea**, which can be combined with a visit to **Masada**, one of Israel's most moving historic sites, where a band of Jewish Zealots made a last brave stand against the Romans in AD73. A day in Masada is a vital piece in the complex jigsaw puzzle that makes up Israel's history and is just as important as the antiquities in Jerusalem itself.

DON'T MISS

★★★ Bethlehem: see where the Christian story began – but explore the town, too.
★★★ Masada: both a moving experience and a significant piece of history.
★★★ Baha'i Shrine: Haifa's stunningly beautiful shrine and gardens.
★★ Floating on the Dead Sea: everybody should try it once.
★ Haifa's café society: make time for a long lunch in the sunshine.

Opposite: *Take the cable car up to the top of Masada, a popular day trip from either city.*

BABE IN A MANGER

In Bethlehem's Church of the Nativity, the **Chapel of the Manger** is where Mary placed the baby Jesus in a manger. The reality, experts agree, is that Jesus was born not in a stable but in a cave or grotto similar to this; many houses in Bethlehem are still built backing onto the hill, which is riddled with caves. What is believed to be the actual manger is now kept in Rome in the Church of the Santa Maria Maggiore.

BETHLEHEM ★★★

Bethlehem is only 11km (7 miles) south of Jerusalem but the difference in scenery is vivid: buildings are run-down and scruffy, the population of 25,000 comprises mainly Muslim and a minority of Christian Arabs and there is graffiti everywhere, Israel's towering **Separation Barrier** a sobering reminder of the constant state of conflict people live in here. Having said this, the little town is worth exploring for its narrow lanes, authentic Arab souk (market) and friendly cafés offering Palestinian dishes accompanied by strong, gritty coffee and maybe a hookah pipe. Try to spend at least half a day here; most organized tours only allow a very brief visit.

Church of the Nativity ★★

A solid-looking structure on **Manger Square** (today a parking lot surrounded by souvenir stalls), the Church of the Nativity, or at least its original basilica, dates back to AD325, and was built by the Emperor Constantine. Emperor Justinian later rebuilt it in the 6th century. Jut like the Church of the Holy Sepulchre in Jerusalem, the Church of the Nativity is too important a spot for only one denomination to occupy, and so there are Greek Orthodox, Armenian and Franciscan sections in this solemn place of worship.

In the sombre gloom, gold-coloured lamps hang from the thick wooden ceiling and parts of the wooden floor gape open, revealing the old mosaics underneath. The tiny

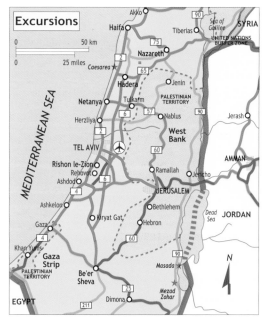

Grotto of the Nativity is down some dark stone steps, with a faded mosaic on the altar and a silver star on the floor marking the spot where Jesus is said to have been born. Open 06:00–18:00 daily.

Milk Grotto ★

Along Milk Grotto Street, which leads off Manger Square, is a limestone cave of important religious significance. Legend

has it that while Mary and Joseph were preparing to flee Bethlehem, some of Mary's milk splashed on the floor as she was nursing the baby, whitening the red rock. Nowadays, both Christians and Muslims believe that a visit to the cave will increase fertility and promote better breast-feeding. Little packets of white stone are sold by the souvenir vendors. Open 08:00–11:45 and 14:00–17:00 daily.

MASADA ★★★

An easy day trip from Jerusalem, this 2000-year-old fortress in the desert was built by King Herod. After the destruction of the Temple in Jerusalem in AD70, a group of Jewish rebels escaped the Romans and fled to Masada where they set up home with their families. In AD73, however, the Romans laid siege to Masada, constructing a massive rampart up the mountainside to the fortress and breaching its walls. You can still see the rampart today.

Refusing to surrender to the Romans, the 1000 Zealots chose 10 men, by drawing lots, to kill the entire population. The 10 then took their own lives, thus rendering the Roman 'victory' a hollow one. Their bravery and determination is a symbol to Israelis today of the spirit of the Jewish people.

Above: *The Church of the Nativity is important to Christians as it marks the spot where they believe Jesus to have been born.*

FINDS IN MASADA

Although the Zealots were careful to destroy most of their belongings before their mass suicide, a number of things have been found in the excavations. Pottery and stone vessels, weapons in the form of arrowheads and amphora were discovered, as well as bronze coins and rare silver shekels.

Interestingly, 11 small pieces of stone were uncovered, each bearing a name, believed to be those of **Eleazar ben Ya'ir**, the commander of the fortress, and the names of the 10 men chosen by lots to kill the rest of the population and then themselves.

Above: *Visit the beautiful Baha'i shrine and gardens, recently designated a UNESCO World Heritage Site, in Haifa.*

HAIFA ★★★

The northern capital of Israel, Haifa is an attractive seaside town, built on steep hills rising up from the coast with panoramic views of the beaches to the south and the distant **Golan Heights** to the north. Haifa is best known as a town where no fewer than six faiths coexist peacefully. As well as Jews, Christians and Muslims, Ahmedi and Druze people live here and the town is the world centre for the Baha'i faith. The skyline is peppered with churches and the beautiful **Baha'i Gardens** are the city's most famous landmark. Haifa is also a wonderful destination for lovers of the outdoors, from the sandy beaches to the nature reserves of **Mount Carmel** and in town, the huge array of outdoor restaurants and coffee shops.

Baha'i Gardens ★★★

The gentle Baha'i faith believes in the unity of all the major faiths, tolerance, peace and justice, and its headquarters are the gold-domed **Shrine of the Bab**, an elaborate structure housing the remains of the Bab, prophet of the faith. From here, immaculate terraced gardens cascade down the cliff face, brilliant with banks of flowers, parades of cypress trees and manicured lawns, and illuminated at night. Open 09:00–12:00 daily (inner gardens); 09:00–17:00 daily (outer gardens). Free tours in English daily (except Wednesday) at 12:00.

Elijah's Cave and the Carmelite Monastery ★★

Elijah, the 9th century BC Hebrew prophet, is venerated by Jews, Christians, Muslims and Druze, and the cave on Mount Carmel where he lived and meditated is an important pilgrimage spot. There's an elaborate domed chapel inside the cave today used for many religious events and festivals. Open Sunday–Thursday 08:00–18:00; Friday 08:00–13:00. Above the cave is the beautiful **Stella Maris Carmelite Monastery**, housing wonderful paintings and dazzling Italian marble. The current basilica dates to 1836, although the Carmelite order of monks dates back to the 12th century. Open 06:30–13:30 and 15:00–18:00.

DEAD SEA RULES

Most tours to the Dead Sea include a couple of hours on the beach. Here, you can bob around in the dense, mineral-rich water, reading a newspaper. The water, though, is actually far from pleasant. Don't get it in your eyes, ears or mouth. Don't try to swim on your front or go out of your depth. Don't swim after shaving – the stinging is intense! And always shower thoroughly as soon as you leave the sea.

Excursions at a Glance

Haifa and the north are best enjoyed in spring and autumn. Summers are very hot and humid and winters can be cool, with snow on the Golan Heights. Masada and the Dead Sea are much hotter and drier, with longer shoulder seasons; summer is just too hot but winters are usually dry and fine, if a little cool in January and February. Christmas in Bethlehem is particularly special and a lot of pilgrims make a special journey to celebrate the birth of Christ.

Ben Gurion International, Israel's main airport, is situated 20km (12.5 miles) from Tel Aviv. Both Jerusalem (for Bethlehem) and Haifa are an hour's drive from here. There are direct **trains** from Ben Gurion to **Haifa**; tel: 03 611 7000, www.rail.co.il

To get to **Bethlehem** other than on a booked tour, you have to take either an Arab **bus** (No. 21) or a private *sherut* taxi from the Damascus Gate (Bab el-Amoud) in East Jerusalem via Beit Jala to Bethlehem. There is an Israeli checkpoint on the road to Bethlehem which may cause delays. You must carry a passport. Any tour will pick up a Palestinian guide once through the checkpoint. Tours and *sheruts* may be held up by the need to change vehicles at the check-

point; everything depends on the security situation at the time of your visit here.

The **Haifa Carmelit** is the only **underground railway** system in Israel and has six stations across the city; tel: 04 837 6661. Haifa also has an efficient bus network. You can walk the city, too, using a network of vertiginous staircases leading up and down the mountainside. Pick up a staircase map from the tourist board first and wear comfortable shoes.

The easiest way to combine a visit to **Masada** and the **Dead Sea** is to book a tour through companies like Guided Tours Israel (tel: 772 285 363, www.guidedtoursisrael.com) or Bein Harim, which offers various combinations including **Bethlehem** (tel: 03 542 2000, www.beinharim.co.il). In cooler weather, devoted pilgrims like to walk from Jerusalem to Bethlehem, which takes about two hours (again, remember your passport for the checkpoint).

Bethlehem
Afteem, Manger Square, tel: 02 277 0157.
This legendary falafel shop is the perfect place for lunch on the run.
Abu Shanab, Ring Road, tel: 02 274 2895.
Much-praised grill restaurant using the freshest of meat.

Dar Jdoudnah, off Manger Square, tel: 02 274 3212. Old-fashioned snack bar with pictures of the town as it used to be. Try the pastries filled with wild thyme and cheese.

Haifa
Hashmura 1872, 15 Ben Gurion Blvd, Hamoshava Hagermanit, tel: 04 855 1872. Classical French cuisine in a beautifully restored mansion in the German Colony.
Abu Yusuf, near the port, tel: 04 866 3723. Typical Israeli/Arabic cuisine – falafel, hummus, grills and a massive salad bar.

In **Haifa**, check out the Castra Art, Recreation and Shopping Centre at 8 Moshe Fliman Street, tel: 04 859 000. It's a huge modern complex of galleries, shops and restaurants with a busy cultural programme.

Ben Gurion International Airport, flight information, tel: 03 972 3344.
Tours of the Baha'i Gardens in Haifa: www.ganbahai.org.il
Information on Bethlehem: Open Bethlehem, tel: 02 277 7993, http://openbethlehem.org Excellent site dedicated to the preservation of the city and encouraging wider exploration.
Haifa tourist information: www.tour-haifa.co.il

Travel Tips

Tourist Information

There are Israel government tourist offices in 19 locations around the world including the UK, the USA and Canada. In Israel, most major towns and cities have an information office and there are several in both Jerusalem and Tel Aviv. These include: Ben Gurion International Airport, Entrance Hall, tel: 03 975 4260, open 24/7; Tel Aviv Tourism Association, City Hall, 69 Ibn Gvirol St, tel: 03 521 8500, open Sun–Thu 09:00–14:00; Tel Aviv Tourism Association, Tel Aviv Promenade, 46 Herbert Samuel St, tel: 03 516 6188, open Sun–Thu 09:30–16:30; Jerusalem Tourist Information, Jaffa Gate, Omar Ibn Katab Square in the Old City, tel: 02 628 0403, open Sat–Thu 08:30–17:00; Fri 08:00–13:00; www.thinkisrael.com

Entry Requirements

Visitors to Israel need a valid passport with an expiry date of more than six months away. Check with the Israeli Embassy or Consulate in your country whether you require a visa. Citizens of most countries, including Australia, Canada, South Africa, the USA and the UK, are granted these on entry.

The normal permitted length of stay is three months, though if you are a cruise passenger just visiting for the day, you will simply receive a landing card. On entering Israel, expect to be questioned at length, particularly if you have Arabic stamps in your passport. The process can seem intimidating and the best way to get through it is to be polite and to offer straight answers. The same will happen when you leave Israel; you will be questioned about what's in your luggage before you check it in and it will probably be X-rayed before you even join the check-in queue. Israel has a limited number of entry points. The three international airports are Tel Aviv's Ben Gurion, Eilat's Ovda, and Haifa. Cruise passengers arrive at Haifa or Ashdod, while there are several points of entry by road (see Getting There). If you are planning to visit other countries which may deny you entry if you have an Israeli stamp in your passport, you can ask for the stamp to be placed on a separate piece of paper, although this is offered less readily than in the past. You will also have problems entering the West Bank if your passport is not stamped.

Visiting the West Bank

Many tourists visit the Palestinian West Bank as a day trip from Jerusalem, or in transit en route to the Dead Sea spa resorts, the Negev and the south. Travel within the West Bank is not possible without passing through multiple Israeli military checkpoints. These checkpoints are flash points for violent incidents and have been the scene of several fatal attacks, so be vigilant. Even on a day trip, take ID with you and prepare for delays. For more in-depth travel, you must consult the **Israel Ministry of Foreign Affairs** (www.mfa.gov.il) or bodies such as the British Foreign Office, which has comprehensive advice to UK nationals on its website (www.fco.gov.uk).

Customs

The following don't need to be declared (other items must be declared in the Red Channel at entry points): spirits, up to one litre, plus two litres of wine per person over 17; perfumes, up to half a litre per person; tobacco, up to 250g or 250 cigarettes per person over 17; gifts (excluding above), up to $200 per person. Camcorders, computers and diving equipment must be declared and a refundable deposit paid (Visa accepted). On exit, claim VAT refunds for items bought from shops with the 'tax VAT refund' logo. Antiques can only be exported with written approval from the Antiquities Authority, tel: 02 629 2627. Customer queries tel: 02 666 4000.

Health Requirements

No vaccinations are required except yellow fever if arriving from an infected area.

Getting There

Points of Entry: Most people enter at Ben Gurion International Airport outside Tel Aviv. There are land crossings on the borders with Jordan and Egypt.
By Air: Airlines from all over the world fly to Ben Gurion International Airport, including the national carrier, **El Al;** tel: 03 977 1111, www.elal.co.il More airlines are starting services to Israel as tourism grows and travellers from the UK can now choose between **Easyjet** (www.easyjet.com), which operates three services a day from Heathrow to Tel Aviv, and **British Airways** (www.ba.com). Low-cost airline **Arkia** (www. arkia.com) offers flights from Amsterdam, Paris, Rome and Kiev, while **Israir** (www.israir airlines.com) flies from Berlin, Moscow, Rome and Nice. From the USA, there are nonstop flights from Atlanta, Miami, Los Angeles and New York (both JFK and Newark-Liberty). **Air Canada** (www. aircanada.com) flies nonstop from Toronto to Tel Aviv.
Israel Airport Authority, tel: 03

975 5555; online info in English: www.iaa.gov.il/Rashat/en-US/Airports/BenGurion/
By Boat: A few cruise lines dock at Haifa and Ashdod and a ferry service goes from here to Cyprus. Passengers can board in Cyprus, Greece, Turkey or Egypt and enter Israel through Haifa Port, Tel Aviv, Ashdod or Eilat. Private yachts may moor at four marinas: Jaffa, Akko, Ashkelon and Herzliya.
By Road: Land entry into Israel is possible through Egypt and Jordan. Border crossings are under the jurisdiction of the Israel Airports Authority. There are three points of entry from Jordan: the Yitzhak Rabin Border Terminal at Eilat, tel: 08 630 0555; the Allenby Border Terminal east of Jericho and an hour's drive from Jerusalem, tel: 02 548 2600; and the Jordan River Border Terminal at Beit She'an, tel: 04 609 3415. There is one crossing from Egypt, the Taba Border Terminal at Eilat, tel: 08 636 0999. The type of traffic allowed through these crossings varies according to the security situation, as do the opening times, so check the Israel Airports Authority website when planning a journey: www.iaa.gov.il/Rashat/en-US/Rashot/FAQ/

What to Pack

Even for business, Israelis are fairly casual. Remember your sunglasses, sunscreen and a hat; swimming gear; walking shoes; long sleeves and long trousers or long skirt for entering religious sites. In winter, bring rainwear and sweaters.

GOOD READING

Gilbert, Martin, Israel – A History (Black Swan, 2008). Comprehensive updated history of the State of Israel.
Rosenthal, Donna, The Israelis: Ordinary People in an Extraordinary Land (Simon and Schuster, 2008). Vivid descriptions of real people, dispelling stereotypes.
Harms, Gregory and Ferry, Todd M, The Palestine-Israel Conflict: A Basic Introduction (Pluto Press, 2008). History of the troubled area explained from both sides.
Holy Bible. Only in Israel does the Bible come so comprehensively to life.
Gur, Janna, The Book of New Israeli Food (Shocken Books, 2008). Recipes of traditional Jewish cuisine and dishes bearing all the other influences of Israeli food, from Middle Eastern to African.

Money Matters

The unit of currency is the New Israeli shekel (NIS), divided into 100 agorot. You can bring an unlimited amount of cash or traveller's cheques into the country. Some shops accept foreign currency, although change will be in NIS. Most credit cards are accepted. Most banks have automatic teller machines. Money can also be exchanged at hotels. VAT in Israel is currently 16%, except in Eilat, which is a duty-free zone for tourists. The duty-free shops at Ben Gurion International Airport only take dollars, so don't save shekels for the airport.

Banks open 08:30–12:30
Sun–Fri; 16:00–17:00 Mon
and Thu.

Accommodation

Accommodation ranges from
luxurious five star hotels to
more modest self-catering
establishments. Hotels are
graded from two to five stars
and usually quote prices in
dollars. The top international
chains are represented across
both cities. Israel's hotels are
represented by the **Israel
Hotel Association**, 29
Hamered St, PO Box 50066,
Tel Aviv 61500, tel: 03 517
0131, www.israelhotels.org.il
Although traditional **kibbutz**
communal life is on the decline, there are lots of kibbutz
hotels as part of the Israel
Kibbutz Hotel Chain, which
makes up the country's largest
hotel group. Book each hotel
individually through www.
kibbutz.co.il Tel Aviv has one
kibbutz hotel and there are
several around Jerusalem, but
not in the city centre. There
are **youth hostels** all over
Israel, including two in
Jerusalem, one in Tel Aviv
and one in Jaffa; tel: 1 599
510 511, www.iyha.org.il
The country also has a wide
network of **Christian guest-
houses**, offering more modest
accommodation aimed at
practicing Christians; there's a
list on www.travelujah.com
Alternatively, you can book a
B&B in Jerusalem direct with
the owner via the very useful
site www.bnb.co.il and in Tel
Aviv via www.iha.com which
features B&Bs and short- or
long-term rentals.

Eating Out

Cuisine from all over the world
is available in Israel. Kosher
restaurants – anything from
Chinese to Israeli or international cuisine – are found in all
hotels and in many towns. Such
restaurants serve either meat or
vegetarian and dairy. Pork is
not served in Jewish, kosher or
Muslim restaurants and seafood
is not sold in kosher establishments. Oriental restaurants in
Israel serve Middle Eastern
food, not Asian as the name
might imply. This is great for
vegetarians and meat eaters,
with a huge range of meze
dishes on offer. Many meals in
restaurants are preceded by a
huge array of dips served with
flatbread, so do not over-order,
as these are filling! Travellers
on a budget can do very well
at the ubiquitous falafel stalls,
where pitta bread is packed
with falafel balls and salad.
Tap water is drinkable in Israel
but if you prefer bottled water,
it is also sold everywhere.
During the month of Ramadan,
Muslims fast between sunrise
and sunset, so places like Jaffa
and the Muslim areas of
Jerusalem may be unusually
quiet during the day. Show
respect for this; and do visit
during the evening, when the
atmosphere is quite festive.

Transport

Air: Domestic flights within
Israel are operated by Arkia
Airlines, tel: 03 690 3712,
www.arkia.com Arkia flies
between Tel Aviv Ben Gurion
or Sde Dov and Haifa and
Eilat, as well as operating
low-cost flights to European

destinations. Israir also flies
between Sde Dov and Eilat,
as well as operating low-cost
flights to European cities (tel:
03 510 9589, www.israir
airlines.com).
Road: Israel has an excellent
road network and most major
car-hire firms operate here.
Drivers require an international
driving licence or a licence
written in English or French. To
rent a car you need to be over
21 and hold an international
credit card. There are plenty of
repair garages and petrol stations. Petrol is cheaper than in
Europe but car rental can be
expensive. Parking is difficult
in towns; a kerb marked with
blue and white means you
need a parking ticket, bought
in blocks from kiosks and
tobacconists. Fines and clamp-
ing are strictly enforced.

Taxis are metered and may be hailed on the streets. A *sherut* is a shared taxi, with a fixed price per passenger.

Buses: The bus network is excellent and reasonably priced. Most urban and inter-urban bus services are operated by the vast Egged Bus Cooperative (tel: 03 694 8888, www.egged.co.il). Local and intercity transport in Tel Aviv and surrounding suburbs is provided by the Dan bus company (tel: 03 639 4444, www.dan.co.il) as well as Egged. Timetables are available from tourist information offices and bus stations. To travel from Jerusalem and Tel Aviv to Eilat, you may need to book in advance. Buses do not run from sundown on Friday to sundown on Saturday and on Jewish holidays.

Trains: Israel Railways Corporation has eight routes including a fast connection from Tel Aviv to Jerusalem. Cheaper than buses, train seats can be booked in advance. Trains usually have a buffet car. Trains do not run on Shabbat or on holidays. For information, tel: 03 611 7000, www.rail.co.il

Hitchhiking: This used to be a way of life in Israel and there are even special hitchhiking stations at major junctions. Motorists give priority to soldiers and there can be a lot of competition. Hitchhiking is dangerous nowadays and is not recommended, especially in the West Bank areas, where there is a risk of kidnapping.

Business Hours

Business and shopping hours are usually from 09:00–19:00 Mon–Thu, Sun, some closing between 13:00 and 16:00. On Fridays and holidays, shops close in the early afternoon.

Time Difference

Israel is two hours ahead of GMT and seven hours ahead of Eastern Standard Time.

Communications

Israelis are avid newspaper readers and there are several dozen dailies, most with a political leaning. Journalists enjoy freedom of expression and the newspapers are full of opinion. *The Jerusalem Post* is published Sun–Fri in English,

while the *Jerusalem Report* is a bi-weekly magazine in English. *The International Herald Tribune* is printed six days a week in Tel Aviv and includes the English-language version of *Haaretz*. There are daily and weekly publications in Arabic, French, Spanish and Russian.

TV and Radio: The Israel Broadcasting Authority is government-run and is funded by licence fees on television sets. The main commercial networks are Channel 2 and Israel 10. Most households subscribe to cable or satellite TV. This includes BBC World Service, CNN and Sky, as well as Lebanese Middle East Television in English and Channel 6 from Jordan, which is also in English. There are numerous commercial radio stations, many unlicensed, carrying everything from pop music to ultra-Orthodox programming.

Post: Post office hours are 08:00–12:30 and 15:30–18:00 daily except Fri afternoon, Sat and holidays. Postboxes are red for out of town and international, yellow for local post.

Telephone: The country code for Israel is +972. Israeli area codes commence with a zero (e.g. 02 123 4567), so if you're calling Israel from overseas, drop the zero (e.g. +972 2 123 4567). Israelis have more cellphones per capita than any nationality on earth. Even children have them. If your cellphone and/or handheld wireless device is programmed for international service, it will work automatically in Israel, although roaming charges can be high. Alternatively, cell-

CONVERSION CHART		
FROM	**TO**	**MULTIPLY BY**
Millimetres	Inches	0.0394
Metres	Yards	1.0936
Metres	Feet	3.281
Kilometres	Miles	0.6214
Square kilometres	Square miles	0.386
Hectares	Acres	2.471
Litres	Pints	1.760
Kilograms	Pounds	2.205
Tonnes	Tons	0.984
To convert Celsius to Fahrenheit: x 9 ÷ 5 + 32		

phones can be rented as soon as you arrive in Israel, or you can buy an Israeli SIM card at Ben Gurion Airport. There are payphones throughout Israel. You'll need to buy a Telecart magnetic card to use them – available at newsstands, supermarkets, post offices or at your hotel front desk. Most hotels and many public places have Wi-Fi Internet at fair prices.

Dialling Codes: Jerusalem 02; Tel Aviv 03; Haifa 04; Galilee and the north 04; the south including Eilat and Be'er Sheva 07; Ashdod 08; Herzliya and Netanya 09.

Electricity

Electric current is 220v AC, single phase, 50 Hertz. Plugs are three-pronged round pin; you'll need an adaptor.

Weights and Measures

Israel uses the metric system.

Health Precautions

The biggest health risk is sunstroke and dehydration. The sun in Israel is most dangerous between 10:00 and 16:00.

Health Services

Israel has an excellent medical system but visitors need private medical insurance as costs can be high. Doctors will come to hotel rooms or can be visited at an emergency room at a Magen David Adom (similar to the Red Cross) Hospital. For an ambulance, dial 101. Pharmacists operate on a rota, the schedule for which is published in the *Jerusalem Post*. Many speak English. You need a prescription for stronger drugs.

Personal Safety

Petty crime – theft, mugging and car crime – does happen, although much less so than in other world capitals and big cities. Violent crime is much less common. Visitors can feel secure wandering around the cities at night. But don't flash wealth around ostentatiously and don't leave anything valuable in a car or hotel room. Security is the biggest issue; report any suspicious packages and never leave bags lying around because they will be blown up immediately. Take note of travel advisories issued on the security situation on the West Bank and Gaza and do not visit if advised against it.

Emergencies

Police, tel: 100
Ambulance, tel: 101
Fire Brigade, tel: 102.
There's a special tourist police division of the police force which deals with everyday matters affecting travellers.

Etiquette

Tipping in restaurants is usually 10–15%. Taxi drivers appreciate but do not expect a tip, while *sherut* drivers need not be tipped. Conservative dress is essential for visiting religious sites. Men should wear a *kippa*, or skullcap; in many places, like the Western Wall, one is provided. Shoes should be removed when entering a mosque. Topless sunbathing is frowned upon. Israelis are generally very direct and open and may strike up a conversation with a stranger in any public place or restaurant. Learn to

embrace this attitude rather than shy away from it; the questions may seem personal but this is the Israeli culture! Respect the Sabbath. Everything starts to wind down on a Friday afternoon and, in Jerusalem in particular, will grind to a complete stop. In a kosher hotel restaurant, the breakfast coffee and bread on a Saturday will have been made the day before (so for a decent Saturday breakfast, find a non-kosher place). Don't ask observant Jews to do anything like attend a business meeting on a Friday afternoon. Do not expect to get anything done on a Jewish holiday (even El Al doesn't fly). When checking in for an El Al flight or crossing borders, don't be offended by rigorous questioning; it's nothing personal.

Language

Hebrew is the official language, along with Arabic. English is a second language in schools. French, Spanish, German, Yiddish, Russian, Polish and Hungarian are widely spoken. Road signs appear in Hebrew, Arabic and English.

INDEX

Note: Numbers in **bold** indicate photographs